Paul

CLARENCE E. MACARTNEY

Paul

Lives of the Old and New Testaments

kregel
PUBLICATIONS

Grand Rapids, MI 49501

Parallel Lives of the Old and New Testaments
by Clarence E. Macartney

Published in 1995 by Kregel Publications, a division of Kregel, Inc., P.O. Box 2607, Grand Rapids, MI 49501. Kregel Publications provides trusted, biblical publications for Christian growth and service. Your comments and suggestions are valued.

Cover Photograph: Copyright © 1995 Kregel, Inc.
Cover and book design: Alan G. Hartman

Library of Congress Cataloging-in-Publication Data
Macartney, Clarence Edward Noble, 1879–1957
    Parallel lives of the Old and New testaments / Clarence E. Macartney.
        p.   cm.
    Originally published: New York: Fleming H. Revell Co., 1930.
    1. Presbyterian Church—Sermons. 2. Sermons, American. I. Title.
BS571.M23   1995   220.9'2—dc20   95–23226
                                                    CIP

ISBN 0-8254-3280-4

1 2 3 4 5 Printing / Year 99 98 97 96 95

Printed in the United States of America

CONTENTS

INTRODUCTION

The many biographies published today, and the great interest shown in them by the reading public, is a testimony to the fascination of biography. Nowhere is this charm so felt as in the Bible. The greatness of the Bible centers around its great characters, and reaches a climax in the greatest of them all, Jesus Christ.

Contrast and comparison serve to bring out the salient features in different characters and personalities. To know what the east is, one must know the west; and one would hardly know what the day is, if one had never seen the night. So when we lay one character alongside another, we can better understand both of them.

My plan in these chapters has been to take a character from the Old Testament and one from the New Testament, give a brief sketch of their careers, and then compare and contrast the two lives. We have an example of this kind of comparison in Plutarch's *Parallel Lives*, where the great biographer compares and contrasts twenty-three Greek characters with twenty-three Roman characters; but, so far as I know, this has never been done with the characters of the Bible.

CLARENCE E. MACARTNEY

1

DAVID AND PETER

When Dante visited Paradise, he related how hope, which awakens love, came to him and said:

> Its effulgence pure,
> From many a star descends; but o'er me fell
> The earliest radiance that my heart can trace
> From his sweet songs—the Bard of Israel.

Not only great poets, but multitudes of believers have felt the radiance that has come from the songs and from the life of David. David—what a name it is! Strange that more men do not call their sons David. The very sound of it is musical, and the name itself sets to vibrating all the chords which God has strung in the heart of man. According to an old rabbinical legend, the harp of David hung over his couch. The night wind playing upon the strings made such pleasing music that David arose from his bed, and all through the night, until the morning came, united words to the music. This legend embodies the idea that in the Psalms of David we have all the music of which the human heart is capable.

Men fail, but not the purpose of God. When Saul rejected God and was rejected by God, Samuel was sent to anoint David as his successor. When he came to the house of Jesse, seven of Jesse's sons passed him in review. They had not even thought it worth while to bring in their youngest brother, who was keeping sheep in the field. When Jesse expressed surprise at the request that David be brought in, Samuel said: "The Lord seeth not as man seeth; for man looketh on the outward appearance, but the Lord looketh on the heart." Back of all heredity, training and environment is the mysterious purpose of God. In the heart of David there was always something which God liked. Therefore He chose him.

During the long period of David's persecution at the hand of Saul, the silver lining of this dark cloud is the friendship of David for Jonathan. When David was discouraged, and beginning to lose his faith, and was in danger of making shipwreck of his career, Jonathan went to him in the wood of Ziph and strengthened his hand in God. This is always the greatest service one friend can do to another. Rare among human friendships, the friendship of David and Jonathan is immortalized by one of the most beautiful monuments of all time, the magnificent elegy which David sang when Saul and Jonathan fell on Gilboa.

In his sermon on the Day of Pentecost, Peter declared that David was a prophet, and that, in Psalm 16, he had foretold the resurrection of Christ. Christ also declared that David spoke by the inspiration of the Holy Spirit when he called Him "Lord." To David was given the promise of an endless line and an everlasting kingdom. God said to him: "Thy kingdom shall be established forever." This promise echoes in the Psalms; notably in Psalm 72.

David was past his noonday when he fell into what he calls "the great transgression," with its fearful and triple crime. When we consider the fall of David, we must remember that he had no barriers to hold him in check, such as restrain men from similar crimes today; that is, constraint of law, the fiat of society, and the pressure of public opinion. As a monarch, he was irresponsible. Nevertheless, the Bible treats his sin as a great sin, and it is quickly and greatly punished. For the moment, passion had dethroned reason and conscience. Yet the fear of God in the heart of David was never quenched, not even by this terrible crime.

We could almost wish that David had died before he fell into this sin. O David, why did you not die, fall yourself in battle, before this dreadful night! The glory and the splendor of your reign are past; now comes the eclipse and the night. If you had died before this triple crime, your name would have come down to us unstained. But now, sufferings and misfortunes await you. Never shall the sword depart from your house. If only you had died before your eyes beheld Bathsheba, before you wrote the letter that murdered Uriah, you would have never seen incest among your own children; Tamar dishonored and Amnon murdered; the bloody dagger of Absalom pass like a curse before your eyes! Never would you have forsaken your capital to hear the curses and execrations of Shimei, nor have cried out, there on your face in the chamber over the gate, with the tears bathing your aged cheeks: "O my son Absalom, my son, my son Absalom! would God I had died for thee, O Absalom, my son, my son!"[1]

But that is an afterthought. It is not possible for us to say when a man ought to die. Had David died before he fell into this sin, the Bible would be without one of its greatest chapters in man's repentance and God's mercy. For David's good and our own this story is related.

> Not in their brightness, but their earthly stains,
> Are the true seed vouchsafed to earthly eyes,
> And saints are lowered that the world may rise.

If it had been some heathen or Oriental king to whom Nathan dared to tell this parable of the ewe lamb, he would have had his head cut off. The great thing about David is that he did not destroy the prophet who rebuked him, but repented. The divinest thing in man is repentance, and great was the repentance of David. Voltaire is said to have attempted to write a profane parody of Psalm 51—David's psalm of repentance after his great sin—but was overcome with shame and confusion, and abandoned the blasphemous project. In his

---

1. See Macartney's *Parables of the Old Testament* (Grand Rapids: Kregel Publications, 1995).

prayer of repentance David said: "Restore unto me the joy of Thy salvation. . . . Then will I teach transgressors Thy ways." This prayer was grandly answered. The Bible has no greater teacher of the power of sin and the power of forgiveness than David.

David was a man of impulses, a man of the heart. This fact is set forth in the words of eloquent Edward Irving: "But the form of his character was vast; the scope of his life was immense. His heart was often strained, and every angel of joy and sorrow swept the chords as he passed. But the music was always breathed of heaven. Such oceans of affection lay within his breast as could not always slumber in the breasts of a hundred men, yet here struggled together in the narrow continent of one single heart."

PETER

Around the dome of Christianity's greatest church one reads the words, "Thou art Peter, and upon this rock I will build My church." Protestants do not interpret these words as do the Roman Catholics. Nevertheless, we all recognize the appropriateness of having Peter's name engraved upon the dome of Christianity's greatest church, for by reason of his deep humanity, Peter is the most representative of all the apostles.

We have no word of his early life; but together with John and James he seems to have been under spiritual influence, and was probably a follower of John the Baptist. After he had been brought to Christ by his brother Andrew, he received his definite call one day in the fishing boat. But he realized his sinfulness and, falling at the feet of Christ, amid the nets and the fishes, cried out, "Depart from me, for I am a sinful man." Peter had always two prime qualifications for Christian leadership and apostleship: he knew he was a great sinner and that Christ was a great Savior. Peter is always named first in the catalog of the apostles, and his activity and zeal justify that preeminence. It is interesting to note that the confession that He is the Son of God and the Messiah, Jesus draws, not from the mystical John, or the melancholy Thomas, or the Hebraic Matthew, but from Peter, the most human, ordinary, and everyday sort of man and, therefore, the most representative of mankind in general.

With James and John, Peter had special opportunities and privileges. He was one of the inner circle of Christ's friends, for as David had his first and mighty three, so had the Son of David. As one of these three, Peter witnesses the transfiguration and the agony of Gethsemane. Always he is a man of impulsive speech and action. When he hears the call of Christ he falls impulsively at His feet and beseeches Him to depart from him. When he sees the glory of Christ on the Mount, and sees Moses and Elijah, he wants to build a tabernacle and stay there forever. When he sees his Lord menaced by the mob and insulted by a slave, he draws his sword to avenge the injury. Yet within an hour or two he is denying that he had ever known Christ. When John hesitated at the door of the empty sepulcher, Peter, with characteristic energy, entered in and gave John the evidence of the Resurrection.

Peter was "consistently inconsistent." He hails Jesus as the Son of God, and the next moment tries to dissuade Him from His redemptive work, bringing upon himself the rebuke, "Get thee behind Me, Satan!" He believed that Jesus could support him on the swelling waves of Galilee; but his faith fails him when he finds himself beyond the safety of the boat. He protests against Jesus washing his feet, and then wants Him to wash not his feet only, but his hands and his head. He boasts that, though all should forsake Jesus, he would be found faithful, and then he denies Him. He cuts off the ear of Malchus in the Garden and then forsakes Jesus. After his vision on the roof of Simon the tanner, he casts off his Jewish prejudices; but after fraternizing with the Gentile converts at Antioch, withdraws from their company when "certain from James" came down, fearing the censure of that pillar of the church and his influential party.

Even the Peter of fiction and legend is represented as a man of persistent but noble inconsistency. A few days before the time set for his execution at Rome, he bribed the jailer and escaped from the Mamertine prison. But outside the gates of the city he met his Lord bearing a cross. To Him the surprised Peter said, *"Domine, quo vadis?"* ("Lord, whither goest Thou?") Jesus answered, *"Venio Roman iterum crucifigi."* ("I go to Rome to be crucified again.") Thus warned and humbled, Peter went back to Rome and presented himself to his jailer to be crucified head downward. Despite these inconsistencies, Peter holds our affection and our admiration. He deserved the stinging and humiliating rebuke administered to him by Paul at Antioch for refusing to associate with the Gentile Christians, and we cannot think of Paul so acting. Nevertheless, Peter is so transparent in his character, so absolute in his actions, both for good and for evil, that we never lose interest in him, and his very inconsistencies commend him to us; for if we take the measure of our Christian life, most of us will find that we fall into the class represented by Peter rather than into that represented by the superior and magnificent Paul.[2]

Peter's great transgression was, if anything, worse than that of David, and his penitence is hardly less wonderful and beautiful. In fulfillment of Christ's promise, "When thou art converted, strengthen thy brethren," Peter became the apostle of boldness and courage. When the rulers of Jerusalem saw his boldness, they took note of him that he had been with Jesus.

COMPARISON

At first these two men appear to have little in common. David was a king; Peter was a fisherman. David was a poet; Peter was a street preacher. David was a conqueror; Peter was a missionary.

Yet there is much in one which suggests the other. Both David and Peter introduce a new epoch in the history of grace and redemption. David stands at the beginning of the kingdom of Israel; Peter at the beginning of the Christian church.

Both David and Peter owed a great deal to friendship; David to Jonathan, Peter to Andrew. Both men committed great transgressions and were guilty of great acts of disloyalty to God. Yet both greatly repented, and the moan of their repentance echoes through the ages. Both are great examples of the mercy of God, and how God can forgive and restore the sinner.

---

2. See Macartney's *He Chose Twelve* (Grand Rapids: Kregel Publications, 1993).

David and Peter were both men of the heart. "The most dangerous disease of the heart is cold." Neither David nor Peter ever show the least symptoms of this disease.

David and Peter were both men after God's own heart. When this is said of David, it does not mean that God did not greatly abhor and punish David's sins, but that, especially in contrast with Saul, David was a man who desired to do the will of God. This was true also of Peter. Both men sinned greatly, but never lost their hold on God. Both could sing the song, "Rejoice not against me, O mine enemy: when I fall, I shall arise."

David, although he was not permitted to do the actual building of the temple, was nevertheless its real planner, maker and builder: whereas Peter, more than any other, is the builder of the Christian church, of which the temple was the type, as David was the type of Christ.

The history of these two men shows how God looks on the heart. Man, who looks on the outward appearance, would have rejected both David and Peter. But God looks on the heart. Therefore it is, strange as it may seem to man, that a murderer and an adulterer were chosen by God to prepare for the building of the temple and for the coming of Christ, and a braggart and a coward to be the chief builder of the church.

Both David and Peter are monuments to the power of temptation, and the power of sin, and both in their terrible fall warn men today. The history of David and Peter says to men today: "Let him that thinketh he standeth, take heed lest he fall." They show us how no religious office, however high, no familiarity with religious things, no entertainment of pious sentiments, no association with religious people constitute in themselves a guarantee against temptation and sin. Yet both men are monuments to the grace of God; and if they warn us against sin, they encourage us in repentance and faith.

I wonder how it will be when David meets Peter in heaven? David could tell Peter much that Peter, and we, too, would like to know; all about Saul, and Samuel and Solomon, and just exactly what he meant in Psalm 22, which Christ quoted on the cross, and in Psalm 16, which Peter quoted on the Day of Pentecost. Peter, too, could tell David many interesting things: all about Christ and the days of His flesh, the Crucifixion, the Resurrection, the Day of Pentecost, St. Paul and the spread of the gospel. But there was one thing which they had in common, and which, no doubt, will be the theme of their conversation. Both were sinners saved by grace, and I doubt not that when the music of heaven's song was first heard by them—"Now unto Him that loved us and hath washed us from our sins by His own blood"—both David and Peter, looking toward the Lamb upon the throne, remembered a great transgression, a great deliverance, and a great salvation.

2

MOSES AND PAUL

MOSES

According to an old Hebrew legend, the supreme angels were commanded to take away the soul of Moses. One of them was Zangziel. But he was afraid to touch Moses, and said, "O Lord, I was the instructor of Moses. How can I take away the soul of my disciple?" Then the Angel of Death drew his mighty sword and approached Moses. But when he saw inscribed on his staff the ineffable Name of the Almighty, and a wondrous luster shining forth from his countenance, for his face shone like the sun, the Angel of Death, too, was afraid, and fled from his presence. Once again he returned, only to be put to flight again when Moses touched him with his staff, upon which was inscribed the ineffable Name. But again the mysterious voice cried out: "The end of thy time hath come. Contend not. Thy life lasteth only a short moment." But Moses answered: "Thou Lord of the universe, who wast revealed to me in the burning bush, remember that Thou didst carry me up into Thy heaven, where I abode forty days and forty nights. Have mercy upon me, and hand me not over into the power of the Angel of Death." The prayer of Moses was granted; the Angel of Death had no dominion over him. But the Almighty, with a divine kiss, removed the soul of Moses.

The mysterious end of Moses on "Nebo's lonely mountain" was a fitting conclusion to his great life. If God's glory hid him at the end of his life, God's providence cradled him at the beginning. God's purposes are hard to stop. Pharaoh tried to stop the purpose of God, and keep Israel helpless and enslaved by throwing every male child into the Nile. But the very river which was to become the grave of Moses became his cradle. The midwives feared God, and a mother's and a sister's love hid the child from the hand of Pharaoh.

What would have happened if Pharaoh's daughter had come to bathe fifty yards further up, or further down, the river, instead of at that spot where the three-month-old babe lay on his back in his creel among the flags, laughing and grasping at the reeds as they swayed and tossed in the afternoon wind? Only the human mind raises that question of an "if." There are no "ifs" in God's eternal purposes, and no accidents in the long chain of His providential decrees. Rocking in his cradle of bulrushes, the future deliverer of Israel was as safe as if he had been sleeping in the palace of a king.

Brought up in all the lore of the Egyptians, the day came when Moses had to choose between Israel and Egypt, whether he was to be a leader of God's people in the desert, or a king on his throne; a builder of nations, or a builder of pyramids; an unknown grave on Pisgah's mountain, or a wrapped mummy in an Egyptian sepulcher.

The crisis of his decision was that day when he saw an Egyptian smiting an Israelite, and himself smote back and slew the Egyptian. This was a greater crime than murder, because he had hid the body, thus preventing it from receiving the elaborate rites of Egyptian sepulture, so that it might gain an entrance into the land of the blessed. That blow which slew the Egyptian was the signature of Moses to the manuscript and affirmation of his life's choice. "By faith Moses . . . refused to be called the son of Pharaoh's daughter; choosing rather to suffer affliction with the people of God than to enjoy the pleasures of sin for a season; esteeming the reproach of Christ's greater riches than the treasures in Egypt."

Out in Midian, whither he had fled, Moses one day saw the shepherds driving the sheep of the seven daughters of Reuel away from the watering place. Once again he lifted his arm on behalf of the oppressed. There is no doubt that Moses has at least one qualification for a national deliverer: he cannot see others suffer injustice without suffering himself. He was called in the Scriptures "the man of meekness," "as meek as Moses." But we have an altogether wrong conception of the character of Moses if we think of him as a weak and placid sort of man. If anything is certain about him, it is that he was violently provoked when others were the object of injustice, and warmly resented injuries done either to man or God. This trait we read in the blow that slew the Egyptian; in his deliverance of the daughters of Reuel from the Midianite shepherds; in his smashing the tables of the law, when he came down from the Mount and found the people worshiping the golden calf; in his smiting the rock twice and denouncing the people for their rebellion at the Waters of Strife. The only time that Moses was mild and meek was when the wrongdoing was directed toward himself. If he was angry at Pharaoh once, when that monarch told him to see his face no more, it was more because of the insult offered to God, than to Moses himself. Although he denounced the people for their idolatry and rebellion, he tenderly interceded for them when they renounced his authority; and when Miriam had been smitten with leprosy, because of her offense against him, when, together with Aaron, she presumed to rebuke Moses for marrying a Cushite woman, Moses tenderly interceded for her, saying, "Heal her, O God, I beseech Thee."

After forty years in Midian, Moses must have thought that life held nothing for him but the keeping of sheep. But during those years of waiting, in the long days with their unbroken quiet, and in the deep silence of the starlit desert nights, God was training Moses in the school of solitude for the great work of emancipator. We cannot understand all that the burning bush means, any more than we can understand the glory of the light that smote Paul on the road to Damascus. That a bush should burn, and yet not be consumed, was indeed a strange thing, and Moses said: "I will now turn aside, and see this great sight." If God was to impress a man with His power, and call him to deliver His people, in some way He had to break through the ordinary and the usual, and say to him, "I am God." Who shall say that God, who makes the sun burn, yet not consume, could not make a bush burn unconsumed? "When the Lord saw that he turned aside to see, God called unto him out of the midst of the bush." God was waiting for a man who could believe in the supernatural, and hear something else than the bleating of the sheep or the herdsman's cry to his flock. Then it was that God gave Moses the great commission to deliver Israel. Moses saw himself standing in the presence of Israel, and saying, "The God of your fathers hath sent me unto you," and the people of Israel asking him, "What is His name?" For this emergency, God provided by giving him His ineffable Name, "I AM THAT I AM." This nameless Name is ever afterward the authority and the inspiration of the great life of Moses. "He endured," says the author of the great chapter on faith in Hebrews, "as seeing Him who is invisible."

In the long duel with the heart-hardened Pharaoh, Moses at length comes off victorious, with the ultimate and terrible miracle, the death of the first-born. Thenceforth he appears in a grand and heroic role as the leader of the Exodus, the chief hero in those great series of events which are fixed forever in the minds of men, the Red Sea, the pillar of fire and cloud, the smitten rock, the armies conquered by prayer, and the ground white with the manna from heaven. A great leader with a great conviction and a great love for his people, and a great faith in God, takes a fugitive horde and transforms them into a nation.

The law came by Moses. That event casts but a few shadows of its grandeur across the pages of holy writ. The Jews came to Sinai a trembling army of fugitives. They left it the destined deliverers, emancipators and teachers of mankind. This was because God made known His ways to Moses, and His acts to the children of Israel, when the earth quaked and the mountain smoked. With Moses, God spoke mouth to mouth. To most prophets, God made Himself known in a vision, or in a dream; but Moses was granted a higher sort of revelation: "My servant Moses is not so, who is faithful in all my house. With him will I speak mouth to mouth . . . and the similitude of the Lord shall he behold." Until God came Himself in the incarnation of Jesus Christ, He came closer to man, and spoke more directly to man through Moses than through any other.

The great question of all religion is this: Has God come out of the silence and darkness and mystery and spoken to man? If so, have we an account of what He said? Until Christ, the great answer is Moses. The law came by Moses, but grace and truth by Jesus Christ.

The forty years of wandering are over; the sieges, the battles, the judgments, the transgressions, the pleadings, the prayers of intercession, the exhortations, the flames of righteous indignation, the marvelous love of Moses for his people, and his tender shepherd's care for them—all that is over. In their camps about the Ark of the Covenant, at the very gates of their goal, the Promised Land, with their standards waving in the morning sunlight, lie the twelve tribes. Beyond the river is Canaan, that land of pure delight and pure desire; while Jordan rolls between. The stage is set for a triumphal crossing, with Moses at the head of the nation. What a conqueror's entry that will be! But God's ways are not our ways.

The people will pass over, but not Moses. The Lord said to Moses, "Get thee up into the top of Pisgah, and lift up thine eyes westward and northward and southward; and behold with thine eyes, for thou shalt not go over this Jordan . . . because ye trespassed against Me among the children of Israel at the waters of Meribah." To us, that seems a pardonable offense, hardly enough to keep him out of the Land of Promise. God, who loves Moses, and who will honor him in his death, yet judges him and closes against him the golden doors of the Land of Promise. Cardinal Newman has beautifully spoken of Moses and his sin:

> Moses, the patriarch fierce became
>   The meekest man on earth,
> To show us how love's quickening flame
>   Can give our souls new birth.
>
> Moses, the man of meekest heart,
>   Lost Canaan by self-will,
> To show where grace hath done its part,
>   How sin defiles us still.

> Thou who hast taught me in Thy fear,
>   Yet seest me frail at best;
> O grant me loss with Moses here
>   To gain his future rest.

Buried by the hand of the angels on Nebo's lonely mountain, and permitted only to behold the Promised Land with his eyes, the day at length came when the great prophet "like unto Moses," and of whom Moses wrote, had appeared upon earth, and Moses, in company with another who had heard the Word and seen the glory of God, was permitted to stand upon a mountain of that Promised Land and speak with Christ concerning His decease which He should accomplish at Jerusalem.

PAUL

After wearying ourselves with a vain effort to climb the lofty mountain of Moses' character and life, what strength is left us to scale that other great mountain whose shadow falls so grandly across the pages of the New Testament? The most eloquent of Christian preachers, in the most eloquent tribute ever paid to St. Paul, called him "the heart of the world." After Christ Himself, Paul is the greatest possession of the Christian church. In him we have an incomparable example of Christian character; a great thinker; a great preacher and church builder; and last of all, a mighty evidence of the truth of the gospel. After the Resurrection itself, the most powerful evidence for the truth of Christianity is the life and ministry of the Apostle Paul. The weight of this evidence has been felt in all ages, and is as powerful and significant today as ever. Saul of Tarsus, the fierce bigot, blasphemer and persecutor, became Paul the Apostle, Christ's noblest friend and advocate; and the chief waster and destroyer of the church its chief builder and advocate. From the mind of this once enemy of Christ comes the greater part of the New Testament, the most profound statement of Christian truth, and the most beautiful and winsome presentation of the Christian graces and virtues.

His parents' zeal for what Moses had spoken sent the young

Saul to Jerusalem to sit at the feet of Gamaliel. The young devotee's zeal for that same law of Moses made him an actor in the tragic scene of Stephen's martyrdom. Out of this immense zeal for the law of Moses, and this immense hatred of Christ and His church, Saul was lifted by the voice that spoke to him when the bright light shone on the Damascus highway. Henceforth, the law's great advocate is the gospel's great proclaimer.

Like other great souls, Paul was schooled in solitude, remaining in the desert, perhaps in the very place where Moses saw the burning bush, for three years. Persecuted at Damascus, under suspicion and repudiated at Jerusalem, with every door seemingly closed against him, Paul is led to the gate of his destiny by the hand of Barnabas, who takes him down to Antioch, where the disciples were first called Christians. Thence, on a March morning, in the year A.D. 45, Paul sailed out of that port on the most momentous voyage in the history of the race. Now the gospel, which had been preached in Judea and Samaria, is to be preached to the uttermost parts of the earth. After years of persecution, shipwreck, sickness, bonds and imprisonment, thorns in the flesh and thorns in the soul, loneliness and heartache, the great apostle, in prison at Rome, reviews his past, and says that he has fought a good fight, finished his course, and kept the faith. Not only the crown of the righteous judge, as Paul called it, do we think of as encircling his brow, but that crown which the verdict of Christian ages has been glad to place upon his brow for preeminent honor in service and devotion to that Jesus Christ whom once he persecuted.

COMPARISON

Great men are the children of great epochs. They appear at great crises in human history when God is opening some new chapter in His book of providence and revelation. Moses and Paul were both highly educated; one in the lore of the Egyptians, the other in the Scriptures of the Hebrews.

Both men were called by a miracle in the desert; for Moses, the burning bush; for Paul, the bright light of Damascus. Both showed themselves qualified for their great work by immediate obedience to the heavenly vision. Both were called to tasks of immense difficulty and danger; Moses to go down to Egypt, whence he had fled for his life, and emancipate a race of slaves; to snatch, as it were, the sheep out of the lion's mouth; Paul, notorious for his persecution of the gospel, to preach it to a race who would regard him as the arch traitor and apostate.

Both men were city bred, yet both were trained in solitude—Moses in Midian's desert, Paul in Arabia's silence.

Both men made great renunciations. Moses gave up the treasures of Egypt for the dangers and perils of the Exodus. Paul counted all things to be loss, "rubbish," that he might know Christ.

They were both men of fiery temperament. No one would think of either Moses or Paul as a meek, tame, or placid man. The tables of stone come down with a crash, and are broken into fragments, when the indignant Moses, descending from the Mount, hears the music of the revelers as they dance about the golden calf. Paul's indignant answer flashes in the night at Philippi, when he refuses to accept the invitation of the magistrates quietly to leave the city, and tells them that, having publicly beaten him and Silas, men uncondemned, and Romans, they must now come down themselves and fetch them out. That anger flashes again as he scorches with his burning remonstrance the High Priest who commanded one of the guards to strike him at the trial before the Sanhedrin: "God shall smite thee, thou whited wall: for sittest thou to judge me after the law, and commandest me to be smitten contrary to the law?"

Both, we shall say, owed much to friendship; Moses, not only to men, but to women, for by his side is the gifted Miriam, who sings with him the song of Egypt's overthrow; Paul, less to women and more to men; among whom are Barnabas, Luke, Timothy, Titus, Epaphroditus and Onesiphorus, whose names, he says, are written in the Lamb's Book of Life. But always, the divine friendship was the most precious and powerful influence in their lives. Moses goes down in history as the friend of God, "whom God knew face to face"; and Paul, in every crisis and trial in his life, can say, "The Lord stood by me." Both are men in whom the divine plan for man succeeds.

Both in a sense were sons of disappointment; Moses, as he stood on the lonely windswept mountaintop, surveying the Promised Land which he was not permitted to enter; Paul, who hoped in vain that Christ would come quickly, the second time, to him and to the world.

When Moses appeared with Elijah on the Mount of Transfiguration, the subject of his conversation was the death of Christ. Wherever we open the pages of Paul's epistles, or wherever we hear him speak in that pulpit which dominated the world, the theme of Paul's sermon is Christ and Him crucified. Here the great prophet and the great preacher are one. Christ said Moses wrote of Him. The Lamb of God slain for the sins of the world is the commanding figure in the revelation of worship and sacrifice which came through Moses. It was because the law of Moses had made this so plain, that without shedding of blood there is no remission of sins, that when Christ finally appeared on earth, John the Baptist could cry out, "Behold, the Lamb of God, which taketh away the sins of the world." This great redemptive fact, set forth in the symbols and rituals of the Old Testament worship, and revealed at length in the death of Christ for the sins of the world, was the great theme and inspiration, the hope and the glory of St. Paul, who said, "God forbid that I should glory, save in the cross of our Lord Jesus Christ."

We know what Moses said to Elijah and to Christ on the Mount of Transfiguration—at least, we know what the subject of his speaking was. Nor have we any reason to doubt that that same great theme, redeeming love, will be his theme in heaven. When Moses and Paul converse together in that world beyond the veil of sense, they will have many things of interest to tell one another. Moses can tell Paul of the Red Sea, and that Pillar of Cloud, and that Rock, even Christ, about which Paul liked to speak, and the mysterious voices of Sinai, and the as yet untold secret of his burial on Nebo's mountain. To Moses, Paul can tell much, too—his zeal for the law that Moses gave, the Voice that broke his heart and changed his life on the road to Damascus; his translation into the third heaven, and how the sights that he saw, and things unutterable he heard, compare with what Moses saw and heard on Sinai's smoking mountain;

and then the secret, veiled in the New Testament, of how, at the end, he was delivered up and received his crown. Yet, I think, all those subjects, so engaging to you and me, will quickly be passed over as they come to the one grand theme for redeemed sinners, the Lamb of God that taketh away the sins of the world. We read of Moses singing now and then; but not of Paul. Yet, I doubt not that in that day both will sing. And what a song it will be, the song of Moses and the Lamb! Part of that song written and composed by Moses, and part of it written and composed by Paul. Perhaps all other harps will be still, all other voices hushed, as those two voices blend in the deep harmony of that everlasting song—

And they sing the song of Moses the servant of God, and the song of the Lamb, saying, Great and marvelous are Thy works, Lord God Almighty; just and true are Thy ways, Thou King of saints. Who shall not fear Thee, O Lord, and glorify Thy name? for Thou only art holy: for all nations shall come and worship before Thee; for Thy judgments are made manifest.

3

EZEKIEL AND JOHN THE APOSTLE

Captivity has been the author of some of the greatest books in the world. Some of the letters of St. Paul were written from his prison at Rome. John was a prisoner in a convict camp when he had his vision of the future of the church and the overthrow of the kingdom of evil. The Book of Ezekiel is another great book conceived and born in captivity.

Ezekiel was a priest at the temple at Jerusalem, and was carried into captivity in Babylon by Nebuchadnezzar about the year 597 B.C. This was before the rebellion of Zedekiah and the complete destruction of Jerusalem by Nebuchadnezzar. While a captive in the Hebrew colony on the banks of the Chebar, a canal or tributary of the Euphrates, Ezekiel had the series of visions and delivered the messages recorded in the book which bears his name. The Book of Ezekiel is one of the most difficult and least read of any of the books of the Bible. The Jews had a law that no one was to read it until thirty years of age. Jerome called it "the ocean of Scriptures, and the labyrinth of the mysteries of God." But, like all difficult books, there are great treasures here for the man who enters it. One cannot read this book without receiving the impression that there is a God, and that God is in human life, doing His will in the armies of heaven and among the inhabitants of the earth. Any book, any friend, any speaker, who helps us to hold the

25

faith that life is more than meat and raiment, that soul is more than body, and that these few years of struggle and sorrow in the narrow defiles and crowded arenas of this world do not measure our existence, and that man has to do, not only with himself and with his fellow creatures, but with God, and can say to us that if sin is here, and sorrow and death are here, the Lord also is here—that book or speaker is a treasure for mankind. The key to this many-chambered, richly-decorated and strangely-echoing palace of Ezekiel's prophecy is the last sentence of the book, where he concludes his description of the Holy City, "The Lord is there."

Sitting one day among the exiles, Ezekiel beheld a whirlwind coming out of the north. The great and ominous cloud was circled with coruscations of fire. Out of the midst of this onsweeping and fiery cloud, there emerged the four living creatures. They had the likeness of a man, and every one had four faces and four wings. Their faces were the face of a man and the face of a lion on one side, and the face of an ox and the face of an eagle on the other side. The wings of these creatures were joined together as they swept forward, turning neither to the left nor to the right. Then Ezekiel saw the third act of this strange vision. Each of the living creatures was accompanied by a gigantic wheel, the rims of which were full of eyes. The color of the wheels was like to beryl. Wherever the living creatures went, the dreadful wheels went with them. Overarching all was the likeness of the firmament, and above the firmament a sapphire throne upon which sat the august figure of a man, and round about the throne was a rainbow of glory.

Before this vision of the glory of God, Ezekiel fell prostrate to the ground. Then a voice spoke to him, saying, "Son of man, stand upon thy feet, and I will speak unto thee." Ezekiel was then given his difficult and dangerous commission to preach to the apostate and rebellious people, with full warning as to the opposition and persecution with which he was to meet. Against this the Spirit told him that he would make his forehead as adamant, harder than flint. As a token of his complete obedience to the Word of God, and his sinking of himself in his commission, Ezekiel was commanded to open his mouth and eat the roll upon which were the divine words. Then the Spirit lifted him, bitter and depressed in his spirit, but with the sense of God strong upon him, and left him among the captives by the Chebar's banks. There, for seven days, he sat in silent astonishment, pondering the vision which he had seen. At the end of the seven days, he received a second instruction from the Spirit, in which he was told that he was to be as a watchman of the house of Israel, to proclaim the imminent destruction of the nation. If he declared this judgment plainly, and the wicked turned not from their wickedness, the prophet would have no responsibility for their death. But if he failed to give the warning, and the wicked perished in their sin, the prophet would share in that guilt and punishment. He was not to be as one of the foolish prophets who "follow their own spirits and have seen nothing," but a prophet who has seen the glory of God and has heard His words.

Then follows the series of extraordinary tableaux and pantomime carried out by the prophet, in which he pictures the overthrow of Jerusalem and the coming down of the judgments of God. In many of these recorded prophecies or tableaux, it is almost impossible to distinguish between actual occurrence and what was only figuratively set forth. Few passages of the Scriptures are so thrilling and dramatic as those in which Ezekiel portrays either the fall of Jerusalem or the building up of the new Jerusalem and the restoration of Israel to everlasting glory. Of these visions and prophecies, we shall select just a few to show the movement and majesty of this book.

Perhaps the best known of these visions is that of the Valley of Dry Bones. The prophet was set down in the midst of a vast and dismal valley, where a great battle had once been fought for empire and dominion. Here had waved the standards of the invaders, and there the banners of those defending their native soil; here the squadrons of horse had met in thunderous onset, and there the phalanxes of the foot soldiers. Long ago the tide of battle had rolled back from this now deserted valley. Silence and desolation reigned there, and the bones of the victims of the battle were strewn over the earth like the fallen leaves of the autumn. Years had passed since the trumpet sounded the attack and the retreat. The vultures had done their part, and the rains and the dews and the snows had done theirs; and now nothing but bones, barren and bleached, were left of the once mighty host. Here they lay, rank upon rank, row upon row. Grim skeletons grinned from the helmets which encased them, and rusted and unlifted lances lay across the bones of the hands which had once brandished them in the face of the foe.

Awed and overwhelmed by the ghastly array, Ezekiel stood in silence beholding the terrible spectacle. The Spirit asked him, "Son of man, can these bones live?" With eloquent hesitation and reserve, Ezekiel replied, "O Lord God, Thou knowest." Then he was commanded to prophesy over the bones, and say to them, "O ye dry bones, hear the word of the Lord." Thus says the Lord God to these bones. "Behold I will cause breath to enter into you, and ye shall live." With that, the valley of death shook with a great earthquake, and with a mighty noise the scattered relics came together, bone to bone. Upon the bones the sinews, and upon the sinews the flesh, and upon the flesh the skin. Still there was no breath in these reassembled carcasses. Then, at the command of the Lord, Ezekiel prophesied to the wind, saying, "Come from the four winds, O breath, and breathe upon these slain that they may live." In answer to his supplication, the wind came upon the dead bodies and they lived and stood up on their feet, an exceeding great army. The purpose of the vision was to revive the nation's faith in its great future. Scattered, exiled, prostrate, and lifeless as Israel now seemed to be, there was yet a great future in store for the people of God. This was the main lesson of the Vision of the Valley of Dry Bones. But Christian faith has often made use of this vision and parable to teach, not only the glorious future of the church of Christ, but the doctrine of the resurrection of the body.

Another impressive vision of Ezekiel is what he tells us about Gog and Magog. Ezekiel is commanded to set his face toward Gog, the Prince of Rosh, Meshech and Tubal, and the land of Magog. He declares to Gog how the Lord will move him to march forth with a vast army recruited from the ends of the earth, from Persia and Cush, to the uttermost parts of the north. Like a midsummer storm, this polyglot host will break in invasion over the land of Israel. The bait that lures them to their doom is the supposed riches of this small and war-wasted land. The merchants of Sheba and Tarshish follow in the train of Gog's army, eager to share in the loot and booty. Then an earthquake heralds the wrath and judgment of God. The mountains are shaken down, and all things created tremble. When Jehovah calls for His sword, a panic seizes the grand army, and every man's sword is against his neighbor, while the heavens themselves fight against Gog, raining down on his army an overwhelming shower of fire, hailstones, and brimstone. On all the hills and plains, the dead lie scattered like autumn leaves. The bows and arrows gathered upon the battlefield are so vast in number that for seven years they supply fuel for all Israel, no wood being taken out of the forest all that period. For seven months all Israel does nothing else but bury the corpses of Gog's army. Even the birds of the air are invited to come to the feast of slaughter and eat the flesh of the mighty and drink the blood of the princes of the earth. By this catastrophic victory, Jehovah glorifies Himself among the nations, and henceforth His people dwell in peace in Zion.

Taken only in a literal sense, the prophecy has great difficulties, for it tells us that all Israel for seven months did nothing else but bury the dead from the battle in the mountains, where the composite host of invasion, Scythians, Persians, Armenians, Cimmerians, Ethiopians, and Libyans, fell before the blast of the Lord. According to the estimate of Fairbairn, one million persons, each man burying two corpses a day, would, at the end of seven months of one hundred and eighty working days, have interred three hundred and sixty million bodies!

But we leave these difficult details of the prophecy, and try to catch the breath of triumph which blows so grandly through it. The vision sets forth the implacable hostility between the church and the world. Ezekiel uses the figures of the carnal world—armies, swords, rivers of blood, mountains sown with dead bodies, and the birds of the air glutting themselves on the fallen and decomposing kings and princes. The conflict which the rapt eye of Ezekiel staged upon the mountains of Israel between Gog and the Sword of the Lord, is going on from generation to generation. The battle will not end until Christ is all in all. Satan is to be crushed, and the seed of the woman will conquer.

To a different note is the closing vision of Ezekiel's book, where he pictures the beauty and splendor of the new Jerusalem. He has had a great vision of the city and the temple, and, conducted by an angelic guide, has traversed the city and marked well her bulwarks and measured the temple. At the door of the temple, he beholds the stream issuing from the foundations and flowing toward the east. The angel measures the stream at some distance from the temple, and the waters are only to the ankles; further on, he measures it again, and the waters are up to the knees of Ezekiel as he passed through them; again, he measures them, and the waters are up to his loins; then a final measurement where the river was too deep to ford, a "river to swim in." As he followed the course of the river, he saw many trees with their greenness and shade on either side of the river. Wherever the river flowed, there was vegetation and life. Even the Dead Sea, that monstrosity among inland seas, heavy with salt, and more than a thousand feet below the level of the ocean, had its bituminous waters healed by the temple-born river which emptied a pure life-giving stream into its dark and desolate bosom.

To us, today, that mystic river is a parable and prophecy of the origin, the increase, the blessing, and the glory of the gospel as it has been carried to the world and down the ages by the church of Christ. With this glorious river making glad the whole earth, Ezekiel's graphic pen and eloquent voice are still. The storm of sin and judgment has passed. He can say of that eagerly-desired city of the future, "The Lord is there."

JOHN THE APOSTLE

John's symbol in church history is the eagle, "kindling his undazzled eye at the full mid-day beam." But there is little in Leonardo da Vinci's famous picture, "The Last Supper," to remind us of the eagle, with its mastery of time and space. He has represented John as a full-faced effeminate youth, with something of a Mona Lisa smile on his lips, his white hands meekly and languidly clasped together, and his head inclined toward Judas, around whose shoulder Peter, with the knife in his right hand, is beckoning to John to ask Jesus whom He meant, when He said that one of them that night should betray Him. There is nothing here to suggest the eagle flying toward the golden gate of the sun, or the Son of Thunder pouring out his woes upon the world.

John is evidently a chief personality among the disciples of Christ. One of the first to be chosen, he was one of the elect three whom Jesus took with Him to the Mount of Transfiguration, and whom He asked to watch with Him in the agony of Gethsemane. At the cross, Jesus commended His mother to the keeping of John, and to John, at length, Christ gave His great vision of the future of the world and the church. Yet in the Gospels, John rarely speaks. He is powerful; but ever within the background and the shadows. His greatness there is a "concealed greatness." There are some men whom we get to know by what they do, or say, or act. Peter is that sort of self-revelatory man. But others we get to know by what they think. In his letters, in his Gospel, and in the Apocalypse, John tells us what he thinks, not about himself, for in his Gospel even his own name is not mentioned, but about Christ. John presents Christ to us under three great aspects—the Divine Christ, the Redeeming Christ, and the Conquering Christ.

Testifying to the Divine Christ, John, in the fourth Gospel, the latest of all his works, and the sunset of inspiration, declares the great mystery of the incarnation, how the eternal Word became flesh and the world beheld His glory. One of the purposes of his Gospel, he makes plain to us, was that as one of the last living witnesses he might testify to Christ as the Son of God, that men believing in Him might have eternal life. In his *Death in the Desert*, Browning imagines what John said when he was dying:

> No one alive who knew (consider this!)
> Saw with his eyes and handled with his hands
> That which was from the first the Word of Life.
> How will it be when none more saith, "I saw"?

We can see, as the contemporary witnesses passed away, how important it was to have the written impressions of a man like John. From the vantage point of great age, John writes in his first Epistle: "That which was from the beginning which we have heard, which we have seen with our eyes, which we have looked upon, and our hands have handled of the Word of life . . . that which we have seen and heard, declare we unto you, that ye also may have fellowship with us."

John testified not only to the divine Christ, God incarnate, but to the redeeming and atoning Christ. The first great fact about Christ is who He is; and the second, what He has done. It matters little what He has done if He is not the Son of God. And, on the other hand, it matters little who He is if He has done nothing for mankind. John presents Jesus in the terms of love; that is, love which atones, love which mediates, love which expiates, love which redeems. "Herein," he says, "is love, not that we loved God, but that He loved us, and sent His Son to be the propitiation for our sins." John, perhaps the only disciple at the cross, is the only one who tells us how a soldier drove his spear into the side of Jesus, and how blood and water came out of the wound. Hence, as long as the church sings,

> Rock of Ages, cleft for me,
> Let me hide myself in Thee;
> Let the water and the blood,
> From Thy riven side which flowed,
> Be of sin the double cure,
> Cleanse me from its guilt and power.

—as long as the church sings that great hymn, it will think of John and his redeeming Savior, the Lamb of God who takes away the sins of the world.

But John sees Christ in a third aspect also—the Conquering Christ. Patmos, an islet in the Aegean, is immortal as the place where John had the vision of the Apocalypse. Byron sang of the Isles of Greece, that "all except their sun has set." But this is not true of one of those islands, historic and sacred Patmos.

A prisoner in the lead mines at Patmos, John, in the spirit on the Lord's Day, had for his introduction to the grand series of visions which were granted to him, a manifestation of the glory of Christ. A voice like that of a trumpet spoke to him, saying, "I am Alpha and Omega, the first and the last." Turning at the sound of the voice, John beheld seven golden candlesticks. "In the midst of the seven candlesticks one like unto the Son of man, clothed with a garment down to the foot, and girt about the paps with a golden girdle. His head and His hairs were white like wool, as white as snow; and His eyes were as a flame of fire. And His feet like unto fine brass, as if burned in a furnace; and His voice as the sound of many waters. And He had in His right hand seven stars; and out of His mouth went a sharp two-edged sword; and His countenance was as the sun shineth in His strength."

When he saw this glorious being, John fell at His feet as dead. Then the glorious figure laid His hand upon him, saying to him, "Fear not; I am the first and the last. I am He that liveth, and was dead; and, behold, I am alive forevermore. Amen; and have the keys of hell and of death." Lifted to his feet, John is told that the seven stars in the hand of the Son of Man are the angels of the seven churches, and the seven candlesticks the seven churches. He is commissioned to write a message to each of the seven churches. Then a door is opened for him into heaven, where a voice is heard, like that of a trumpet, talking with him, and saying, "Come up hither, and I will show thee the things which must be hereafter."

That word spoken by the Voice out of heaven to John, "The things which must be hereafter," is the key to the Apocalypse. Every thoughtful mind will have its times when it turns toward the future. The thought of that future not infrequently haunts us. "Then cometh the end," is just as logical and inevitable as "In the beginning." When we ask ourselves what that end is to be, and how it is to come, our best answer is found in the flaming symbols of the Apocalypse, where, under the guidance of the Holy Spirit, we are permitted to gaze down the long corridors of time and behold the judgment of evil and the triumph of the right. Bossuet has rightly called the inner principle of the Apocalypse the fact that "the Most High has made, not one world, but two, a kingdom of God and a kingdom of Satan." In the Apocalypse of John, what we are beholding is the age-long and truceless conflict between good and evil, the church and the world, the earth and the woman, Christ and Satan. If ever we are discouraged by the apparent slow progress of the gospel, and, as in John's awful vision, "see the Beast coming up out of the abyss, with his death stroke healed, to deceive and betray the sons of men"—a powerful parable of the malignity and reverescence of evil in the world—the best tonic is for us to turn to the pages of the Book of Revelation. We are not to be wise above what is written, and we may not be able in every instance, or in many instances, to give the exact equivalent, in time, historical institution, or personality. Nevertheless, whatever we can or cannot understand in these resounding thunders, reverberating judgments, flying angels, emptied vials of wrath, Satan and his hosts cast into the pit, and the star Wormwood falling from heaven, always on the horizon we can behold the great white throne of that God who is the great Actor on the stage of history, for whom the rise and fall of empires, and all the world movements, are but the brief embodiment of His purpose and the transient expression of His desires. And always, too, coming with the music of redemption and victory, we can behold the White Horse and his Rider, upon whose vesture and upon whose thigh is written, "King of Kings, and Lord of Lords."

COMPARISON

Ezekiel and John both suffered exile for their faith: Ezekiel in Babylon, under the then ruler of the world, Nebuchadnezzar; John at Patmos, under the then ruler of the world, the emperor Domitian. Both of them were men of sorrows and acquainted with grief. Of Ezekiel, we are told that his wife, the "desire of his eyes," died; but that Ezekiel, in obedience to God, put aside all visible demonstration of sorrow that he might discharge his public duty. Of John's inner and domestic life, we know nothing, save that James was his brother, and that of all the disciples, John was the one to whom Christ committed the care of His mother.

Both Ezekiel and John were men devoted to the Word of God; Ezekiel ate the roll, and John ate the little book. And to both of them, the Word of God, thus symbolically received and obeyed, was as sweet as honey.

The prophecy of Ezekiel and the prophecy of John both open with an overwhelming vision of the glory of God. Ezekiel beholds the likeness of the man seated upon the throne of beryl over the firmament, and attended by the four living creatures with their outspread wings, and their faces a composite of the power of creation, the ox, the eagle, the lion and the man; and by their side the awful wheels full of dreadful eyes; whereas John beholds the glorious figure of Christ amid the golden candlesticks with the seven stars in His hand and the two-edged sword flaming out of His mouth. The great careers of these prophets began with a vision of God's glory. The church today needs some few reflections, at least, of that glory, those turning wheels full of the eyes of predestination and power, and that flashing sword. We need to bring the cherubims who veil their faces before God back into our churches. As the glory of God fades, and the sense of His majesty declines, and man is exalted, the popular religion of the day threatens to become the worship of the creatures, rather than the worship of the Creator.

Ezekiel and John are both the prophetic historians of the last great battle in the long warfare between good and evil. Ezekiel pictures this battle in the overthrow upon the mountains of Israel of Gog and Magog, when Jehovah called for His sword, and the multitude of the dead lay like the leaves of the forest when autumn has blown. John describes the same ultimate and decisive battle when Satan, loosed from his thousand-year stay in the pit, stirs up Gog and Magog, whose number is as the sand of the sea, to compass the camp of the saints about and the beloved city. Fire comes down from God out of heaven and devours them. Then, when the sea has given up the dead which are in it, and the dead have been judged, the Devil is cast into the lake of fire and brimstone, and death and hell are finished.

Both John and Ezekiel interpret history as superintended by the mind and purpose of God. In Ezekiel's vision, the rolling wheels of destiny have their rims full of the eyes of purpose and predestination. In the vision of John, the seven-sealed book of mystery, which no man in heaven or on earth can open, is opened by Christ, the Lamb of God. Christ is the key to the history of the world, and toward His final victory all world movements are converging.

Ezekiel's book ends with the great declaration, "The Lord is there!" John's book ends with a vision of the Holy City coming down from God out of heaven, so that men can say, "The tabernacle of God is with men." Both Ezekiel and John describe a city of surpassing and almost unimaginable splendor and glory, Ezekiel presenting to us a city whose dimensions are greater than those of the Holy Land itself; and John answering him with a noble antiphony in which he sings of the Holy City of God with its twelve foundations, in which are the names of the twelve apostles of the Lamb, and its twelve gates of pearl, with the names of the twelve tribes of the children of Israel written thereon. In John's vision, the glorious temple and altar of Ezekiel's city have not disappeared, but rather have been magnificently fulfilled and realized in the kingdom of heaven, wherein the Lord God Almighty and the Lamb are the temple of it.

In both of these visions of the golden age and Messiah's reign, there appears, flowing through the land, a river of Water of Life. Ezekiel, in his vision, saw the mystic waters issuing from under the foundations of the temple, ever swelling in volume and depth, and wherever it goes leaving peace and benediction on its banks and healing the poisoned waters of the Dead Sea of the world's sin and hate. John, in his vision, sees flowing out of the throne of God and the Lamb, a river of water of life, clear as crystal. On either side of the river of life was there the Tree of Life, which bear twelve manner of fruit, and yielded her fruit every month; and the leaves of the tree were for the healing of the nations. When, at length, all that Ezekiel and John foresaw and foretold has come to pass; when Satan's empire has fallen, and Christ is Lord of Lords and King of Kings, and sin and sorrow and death are finished, and we sit down with all the redeemed of Christ upon the banks of that river of Water of Life proceeding out of the throne of God and the Lamb, and sing no longer the songs of captivity, but the songs of triumphant Zion, we shall not forget the two men who, better than all others, let us behold, as in a glass, that coming glory, and, before our day, permitted us to taste its joys and, by faith, enter into its deep and unbroken peace.

4

PHARAOH AND HEROD

PHARAOH

The history of Israel from the time that God called Abram out of Ur of the Chaldees, to the time of Christ, is one long chain of Providence, in which one link of history and human action is joined to another. When we survey the entire chain of events, we can see how each event had its place and its meaning, although, had we been alive, and contemporary witnesses of those events, we might not have understood their meaning and their purpose. Providence is a book which, like the Hebrew Bible, must be read backwards. The Hebrew people have not only played a great part in the history of redemption up to our own age, but, according to the New Testament prophecies, are to play a great part in the future. Their falling away, Paul tells us, was a blessing to the world because thereby the gospel was preached to the Gentiles. He argues that a still greater blessing will come to the church and the world through the restoration of the Jews. We doubt not that that great blessing is even now being prepared by the great Director of the events of time and the great Actor on the stage of history. It is not possible for us to note or describe those events; but when the great prophecy as to the future of Israel has been fulfilled, then it will be seen that certain events, perhaps the events of our own day and generation, played no little part in the divine consummation.

The name Pharaoh, made as familiar to men today as Smith, or Jones, or Brown, because it occurs in the Bible, opens for us a chapter in God's providential dealing with His people Israel. His purpose for the Jews involved the captivity of Israel in Egypt, and their ultimate deliverance. In the captivity of Israel a boy's dream played its part, for it was Joseph's dream of his brothers' sheaves worshiping his sheaf which inspired the enmity and hatred of his brethren, and led to their selling Joseph into Egypt. Again, it was a dream in the prison in Egypt, and Joseph's interpretation of it, which led to his release from prison, and, when he had interpreted the dreams of Pharaoh, to his promotion to the high office of chancellor; and this, in turn, led to the saving of Israel from starvation and the bringing down of Jacob and his sons into Egypt.

But now, after four centuries in Egypt, the time has come for the deliverance of the people and their restoration to their own land. Although in a nominal captivity, the people had greatly prospered. As Stephen put it in his apology, "But when the time of the promise drew nigh, which God had sworn to Abraham, the people grew and multiplied in Egypt." The chronicler of Exodus says of this national growth and prosperity: "The children of Israel were fruitful, and increased abundantly, and multiplied, and waxed exceeding mighty; and the land was filled with them."

It was this very prosperity which led to their oppression. There arose a new king over Egypt which knew not Joseph. This does not mean, of course, a king who did not know Joseph personally, for Joseph had been dead for several hundred years; but that the old tradition of kindness and hospitality to the Jews had been forgotten. This Pharaoh who knew not Joseph is generally supposed to have been Rameses II. He said to his advisers that the prosperity of the children of Israel was a menace to Egypt, and that in a time of war they might join with the enemies of the country. He plans, therefore, to "deal wisely," or craftily, with the people. He does not want to exterminate the race, but to reduce them in vigor and diminish them in numbers.

To this end, he sets over them taskmasters who are to compel them to build the great treasure cities, Pithom and Raamses.

These taskmasters are to afflict them and oppress them in their labor. But this plan of Pharaoh fails utterly. The blood of the martyr has always been the seed of the church, and here the suffering of the Hebrews becomes the strength of the nation. The more they afflict them, the more they multipy and grow. Again Pharaoh makes their lives bitter with hard bondage in mortar and in brick, as they rear for Egypt huge storehouses and other colossal structures.

Frustrated in his first plan, that of reducing them by bondage, Pharaoh now attempts to stop the natural increase of the population by putting to death the male children at their birth. He instructs the midwives that they are to permit daughters to survive, but every male child is to be killed. We cannot be sure from the record whether these midwives were Hebrews or Egyptians; probably they were Hebrews. They feared God, and did not as the King of Egypt commanded, but saved the male children alive. If they were Hebrews, both religion and humanity dictated such an invasion of Pharaoh's monstrous edict. If they were Egyptians, then humanity alone prompted them to such a course. Pharaoh was not only frustrated in his plan, but he was fooled and deceived by the women upon whom he had counted to carry it out.

Foiled a second time, Pharaoh now calls upon the whole Egyptian nation to assist him in his nefarious project. He charges all the people, saying, "Every son that is born he shall cast into the river; and every daughter he shall save alive." But this barbarous edict, too, was one which could not be enforced. The natural course of human history and human instinct was against him. A man of the house of Levi, we are told, took for his wife a daughter of Levi. The Jews still married and gave in marriage, although the dark shadow of Pharaoh's cruel decree hung over this relationship. This natural event, the marriage of this son of Levi to a daughter of Levi, was followed by another natural event, the birth of a child. It must have been with no little anxiety that parents awaited to see whether the child for which they had hoped was to be a daughter or a son. If a daughter, they could set their minds at ease; if a son, they must either mourn his destruction or safely hide him.

The child born to this daughter of Levi proved to be a "goodly" child. We are not told what the father thought, and it is interesting to note that it was the mother's regard for this child, and the mother's plan, which saved him from death for at least three months. At the end of that time, when she could no longer hide him, probably because of his growing size, or the proximity of Egyptians who might report his birth, Jochebed made an ark, or creel, of bulrushes, and daubing it with slime and pitch, put the child therein; and then carried the little craft and laid it in the flags by the river's brink. The going away from home of a son or a daughter for the first time is always an event. Farewells are accompanied with affectionate gifts, counsels, prayers and tears. But what a going away from home was this! The little babe of three months, still a stranger to everything save the haven of his mother's breast, is placed in a boat in the river, subject not only to the perils of the river, but, if discovered, a sure victim to the ferocious plot of the King of Egypt.

We are told that the mother left Miriam on guard, and how, as she was watching at her post one day, the daughter of Pharaoh came down to the river to bathe. If she had come down to the water fifty yards further up, or further down the river, the history of the world might have been different. But there are no "ifs" in the divine plan of God for the world. Like the wheels in Ezekiel's vision, His providences move straightforward. It is a beautiful idyll this, the picture which the Book of Exodus gives us of the babe in his cradle in the river, with the splashing of the waves and the sighing of the wind through the flags for his lullaby.

The daughter of Pharaoh, when she saw the ark, sent a maid to fetch it to the bank, and when she had opened it she saw the child; and the child, seeing these strange faces, began to weep. "One touch of nature makes the whole world kin." The daughter of Pharaoh knew of her father's decree; but the sight of this child, a goodly and beautiful babe, and his frightened cry, opened a fountain of compassion in the heart of the princess. The quick-witted Miriam, sure that these two women meant no harm to her brother, now approached them, and assuming that Pharaoh's daughter intended to save the child, and therefore would need a nurse, said to Pharaoh's daughter:

"Shall I go and call to thee a nurse of the Hebrew women, that she may nurse the child for thee? And Pharaoh's daughter said to her, Go. And the maid went and called the child's mother." Thus Moses was returned to his mother's arms and his mother's care. When he was weaned he was brought to the daughter of Pharaoh's house, and became as her son. It was she who gave him his name, Moses, meaning, "I drew him out of the water." So Moses, saved by the daughter of the king who had decreed his destruction before he was born, is brought up in the household of Pharaoh, trained in all the knowledge of the Egyptians. The great purpose back of all this was made plain forty or fifty years afterward, when Moses, an exile and outcast in the desert of Midian, turns aside to see the bush burn, and is called of God to bring Israel up out of the land of Egypt and out of the house of bondage.

HEROD

The name of Herod is just as familiar as that of Pharaoh, and the two names taken together spell out the inability of man by his devices and his cruelties to arrest or hold back the chariot of God's purpose. Pharaoh recalls the great failure of man to block the purpose of God in the Old Testament times, and Herod, that same failure in New Testament times.

History delights in contrast. But never was there such a contrast as this, the Child in His mother's arms at Bethlehem and the gloomy king of Judea, Herod the Great. Herod had not long to live or reign; yet he was troubled when the Wise Men came from the East and inquired for Him that was to be born King of the Jews. When the chief priests and scribes had located Bethlehem as the predicted place for the birth of the King, the crafty Herod sent them all into Bethlehem, telling them that when they had found the Child, they were to return to Jerusalem and bring him word, so that he, too, could go and worship the new-born King.

Herod helped and guided the Wise Men to the manger cradle at Bethlehem, where the Child lay in His mother's arms. But the crafty plot of the king failed. After they had worshiped the young child, and presented to Him their gifts of gold, frankincense and myrrh, they were about to return to Herod at Jerusalem, and then go on to their homes in the far East. But being warned of God in a dream that they should not return to Herod, they went to their homes by another route. Still the Child was not safe. In another dream the angel of the Lord tells Joseph to go down into Egypt and take his wife and the Child with him. There in that same Egypt, where Pharaoh once sought to destroy the Hebrew nation, the Messiah is safe from the wrath of Herod. When the king saw that he had been mocked and deceived by the Wise Men, his anger knew no bounds, and, in keeping with his sanguinary career, he gave an order that all the children of Bethlehem, and in the country round about, from two years old and under, were to be put to death. By this wholesale massacre, he was sure that he would destroy the rival to his throne. The tomb of Rachel was not far from Bethlehem, and the frantic fathers and mothers, bereft of their babes and stripped of their hopes, fancied that Rachel, the ancestress of their race, was weeping again with them in sorrow over the woes of her people. "In Rama, was there a voice heard, lamentation, and weeping, and great mourning. Rachel weeping for her children, and would not be comforted, because they are not."

This savage and bloody massacre of the children was keeping with what we know from other sources of Herod and his character. A brief catalog of the crimes of Herod would take in the murder of all his rivals of the Hasmonean house, the drowning of his brother-in-law, the High Priest Aristobolus, the strangling of his beautiful queen, Mariamme, whom he so passionately loved, and whose name after she was murdered he so incessantly, tenderly, yet bitterly, called; his three sons, Alexander, Aristobolus, and Antipitar, the order for the execution of this last son having been given as Herod lay groaning on his own deathbed. These are only a few of the bloody deeds of this cruel despot, who seems to have been possessed with a legion of devils. As a fitting climax to this bloody reign, Josephus tells us that when Herod lay dying amid loathsome and terrible misery in his ivory palace at Jericho, realizing that none would lament his passing, and that when he was gone the people would rejoice instead of sorrow, he gave orders that the chief families of the land should be shut up in the hippodrome and be put to death the moment the breath left his own body. Thus he would be sure that there would be mourning in the land when he expired. Fortunately, his sister Salome released the doomed persons who had been shut in the hippodrome and saved them from death. Thus Herod's most bloody ambition was not fulfilled. Yet his cup of iniquity was full enough as it was.

By putting to the sword all children of two years of age, Herod was sure that he was destroying the rival King. But he was mistaken. His cruelty made the streets of Bethlehem run with the blood of the innocents; but the Child whom, above all others, Herod wished to kill, was safe in Egypt. Herod's sword was long and sharp, but not long enough to reach to Egypt, nor sharp enough to penetrate the thick armor of God's providential care.

The worst of men, as well as the best, must die. Herod, too, had to die. So we read, that when Herod was dead an angel appeared to Joseph in Egypt and told him that it was safe to take the Child and His mother and go back to the land of Israel, "for they are dead which sought the young Child's life."

COMPARISON

Pharaoh and Herod were both kings, and both men of great ability and great energy. Both were great builders. Pharaoh built the colossal treasure cities, Pithom and Raamses; whereas, Herod built an ivory palace at Jericho, notable structures at Capernaum, and rebuilt the temple with a splendor which surpassed that of Solomon.

Both were men of great cruelty. Pharaoh ordered the assassination of the infants of a whole nation; and Herod, the murder of the infants of Bethlehem and its surrounding country. Had it served his purpose to destroy the infants of the whole Hebrew nation, he would not have hesitated. Both men sought to deal with what they feared by trying to kill it. Pharaoh tried to check the prosperity of Israel and their fecundity by throwing every male child into the river. Fear and hate know no plan of operation save that of opposition and destruction.

Both the Egyptian king and the king of Judea were men who were found, as Gamaliel put it, "fighting against God."

Pharaoh tried to keep Israel in weakness and bondage. He sought to accomplish this by the murder of the nation's childhood. But the fear of God in the hearts of the midwives, and the instinct of paternity and maternity in the young man and young woman of the house of Levi, and the compassion of Pharaoh's own daughter frustrated the plot of the king who tried to hold back the plan of God. Pharaoh decreed before Moses was born that he should be drowned in the river Nile. Herod decreed the destruction of the manhood of Israel; but God decreed the growth and deliverance of Israel, and this was to be accomplished by the Hebrew child, who, hidden in the Nile, was to be brought up in the very palace of that king who had decreed his destruction. Herod, uneasy, and conscience-stricken on his throne, was determined that no rival king should push him from his seat or succeed to his bloody line. To make this sure, he put to the sword every babe of Bethlehem and the surrounding country. But his decree was as ineffectual as the decree of Pharaoh had been centuries before. Herod decreed the destruction of Jesus after He was born, as Pharaoh had decreed the destruction of Moses before he was born. But the decree of Herod, like that of Pharaoh, was set aside by the decree of God. At the beginning of these two great epochs in the history of redemption, in these two great fragments of divine Providence, we see it plainly written that God's purposes cannot be arrested, turned aside, or frustrated. "He doeth His will in the armies of heaven, and among the inhabitants of the earth. Surely the wrath of man shall praise Thee; the remainder of wrath shalt Thou restrain."

The purpose of God with Israel was the same as when His providence shielded Mary's Child from the sharp sword of Herod. "They are dead that sought the young Child's life," the angel said to Joseph in Egypt, when Herod was dead. Each new age has its successors to Herod who seek the young Child's life. Their purpose is the same from age to age, although new uniforms appear, and new phrases are coined, and new weapons are employed. But ever the contest comes to an end with that verdict of the angel of the Lord, "They are dead that sought the young Child's life." The generations of unbelief come and go, but the Eternal Child lives forever.

5

BALAAM AND JUDAS

BALAAM

Balaam is one of those wandering stars of whom Jude speaks in his brief, but volcanic Epistle. There is no doubt that he was a star; nor is there any doubt that he was also a wandering star, quenched in darkness. His history is such that it could hardly have been forgotten, even had there been no New Testament references to him. But Peter, Jude, and John, all refer to him and hold him up as a warning to succeeding generations.

He is a wandering star; and how difficult it is to follow him in his wandering. A strange, complex, contradictory, paradoxical character he is. But so is every man; and how strange are the devious courses of every human heart. The heart of man is deceitful above all else. Who can know it? Balaam is undoubtedly one of the greatest geniuses of the Bible. He hailed the future of Israel with some of the most magnificent and most familiar prophecies of the Scriptures. The lips of the devout and faithful will repeat them to the end of time: "God is not a man that He should lie; neither the son of man, that He should repent." "Let me die the death of the righteous, and let my last end be like his." "I shall see Him, but not now: I shall behold Him, but not nigh; there shall come a Star out of Jacob and a Scepter shall rise out of Israel." These prophecies tower like mountains among the Psalms and predictions of the Bible. Yet

Peter writes of the "madness of the prophet," and Jude of the "error of Balaam," and John of the "doctrine of Balaam." The two verses which compass the history of Balaam are these: "Let me die the death of the righteous and let my last end be like his." . . . "Balaam, also, the son of Beor, they slew with the sword." His prayer tells us the kind of death he wanted to die; but the record in the Book of Numbers tells us of the wretched death which he did die.

Balak, the king of Moab, when he heard of the approach of the children of Israel, fearing that what had happened to Og, king of Bashan, and Sihon, king of the Amorites, would happen to him, dispatched ambassadors, with the rewards of divination to the far East, clear to the banks of the Euphrates, to invite Balaam to come and curse Israel. The ambassadors came to Balaam and asked him to curse Israel, saying: "He whom thou blessest is blessed, and he whom thou cursest is cursed." Balaam might have gone, pretended to have cursed, taken Balak's cash, and gone home again. But he stands on a higher plane than that. He inquires of Him in whose Name he both blesses and curses. God answered, "Thou shalt not go with them; thou shalt not curse the people; for they are blessed."

When the messengers brought back Balaam's refusal to Balak, that king, going on the principle that every man has his price, sent a second embassy and a caravan with gold, and costly presents. When the second embassy came, Balaam, with feigned indignation, said: "If Balak would give me his house full of silver and gold, I cannot go beyond the word of the Lord my God, to do less or more." The boastful tone of these words, as in the case of Peter's fall, prepares us for what follows. After this indignant protest, Balaam says at once, "Now therefore, I pray you, tarry ye also here this night, that I may know what the Lord will say unto me more." That marks the beginning of his downfall.

Balaam was not a man without conscience—far from it. But it is his attitude toward conscience which makes the story of his life so tragic, and yet so instructive. God had spoken once and plainly. The second embassy came with the same request with which the first had come. Balaam knew this when he invited them to stay overnight. He seems to think that perhaps

God will change His mind. It is a dark day for the soul when a man begins to trifle or tamper with his conscience. A perfectly vicious man would be a devil. There is no such man on earth, for every man is a combination of good and bad. The interesting thing about Balaam is that the veil is lifted from his heart, and we see, as in few lives, the struggle between good and evil, and how a man will shuffle, cheat, lie, deceive himself, in order to satisfy his desires.

Balaam was not true to the light which he had, and that light went out. The light that was in him became darkness, and how great was that darkness. So Christ said, "The light of the body is the eye: therefore when thine eye is single, the whole body also is full of light; but when thine eye is evil, thy body also is full of darkness. Take heed therefore that the light which is in thee be not darkness." Balaam was not true to himself. His eye was not single. In the striking sentence of Frederick Robertson's sermon on Balaam, he would not call white black, but he would sully white until it was black. Balaam is one of the most gifted men of the Old Testament, and Paul one of the most gifted of the New Testament. Yet the difference between them in character and influence is immeasurable. But that difference was only a question of time. When God spoke to Paul he answered immediately, "What wilt thou have me to do?" "Immediately I was not disobedient unto the heavenly vision." When God spoke to Balaam he waited for a second night, hoping that God would speak in a different voice that night. But the same God who had said to him on the previous visit of these messengers, "Thou shalt not go with the men," now said to him, "Go!"

With the first streak of the morning light, Balaam was off toward Moab. If he believed that God permitted him to curse, as well as go, he was only caught in the net of deceit that he had woven for himself. The permission of his own lusting heart was taken for the clear command of God, who has said that with the upright, He will show Himself upright, and with the froward man, He will show Himself froward. The wreckers on the coast of Cornwall used to put out the true shore lights and display false lights that lured ships to their destruction and mariners to their death. Sin is the great soul-wrecker.

It displays false lights, and deceives the soul into thinking that its course is right and will lead to peace.

As the eager prophet, bound for Moab, and bent on filthy lucre, hurries on his way, suddenly, the angel of God stands before him with a drawn sword. What even a dumb ass could see and hear, this man, carried away with the sinful desire, could not see and could not hear. In the words of Peter, Balaam was "rebuked for his iniquity; the dumb ass speaking with man's voice forbade the madness of the prophet." Then the Lord opened the eyes of Balaam, and he saw the angel of Jehovah standing in the way with a drawn sword in his hand. Balaam then said—what? What we all say, what anyone says, when he sees the drawn sword of judgment—"I have sinned, for I knew not that Thou stoodest in the way against me. Now, therefore, if it displease Thee, I will get me back again." But he found it was not so easy to go back as he imagined. The angel of the Lord said to Balaam, "Go." So Balaam went with the Prince of Balak. Not once only on the highway between Mesopotamia and Moab, have man and that angel faced each other. The sequence of sin compelled Balaam to go on; Balaam had gone too far now to turn back. On he must march to the end of the road. A man can go against his conscience over all warnings and obstacles, until the path gets dangerous, and the sword of judgment begins to flash before his face, and then wish to turn back. But he may find, as Balaam did, that he cannot turn back. The current on which he has so eagerly cast himself is now too strong for him to turn against it. Now that the swords of retribution and danger are flashing, he says, "I will go back. I did not know; I did not understand; I did not consider." But the angel of judgment sternly commands, "March on! Go on! Go on to judgment and to death!"

All that henceforth happens to Balaam is only the result of his former disloyalty to the light that God gave him. Although he went with the men, Balak could not persuade him to curse Israel. In terms of incomparable splendor, Balaam, conducted from mountaintop to mountaintop, predicted the glorious future of Israel. For a moment, lifted out of himself as he sees the encampment of the people of God, and beholds with prophetic eye their great future, Balaam wishes for himself the death and destiny of God's children: "Let me die the death of the righteous, and let my last end be like his." But alas, passing emotions and transitory wishes are not enough. He longed for the end and the blessing of the Hebrews, but his life did not square with the wish. Unable to curse Israel, he nevertheless set himself to tempt them to idolatry and sensuality in an abominable and damnable plot, so that Israel would curse itself by its own corruption. Yet, over the black furnace of his heart there sounds the grand music of those blessings and predictions as he surveyed the camp of Israel and beheld their glorious future.

Stirred to the center of his being by his vision of the splendor of Israel's future, Balaam has for the moment a sincere desire to share that great destiny, and exclaims, "Let me die the death of the righteous, and let my last end be like his." But Balaam did not die the death of the righteous. Instead of that, he fell in the battle between the Israelites and their enemies, the Midianites. Unburied, unhonored and unsung, there he lies among the heaps of corpses on the field of battle, where the judgments of God had fallen upon the enemies of His people. Instead of dying the death of the righteous, and having his last end like theirs, Balaam died the death of the unrighteous and fell in the ranks of the enemies of God. "Balaam the son of Beor they slew with the sword."

JUDAS

Once, in the Middle Ages, a young artist wished to secure a model for the child Jesus. After long searching, he found the infant of a peasant woman which met the demands of his conception of the Holy Child, and the picture was painted. Years afterward, when he was an old man, he was to paint a picture of Judas Iscariot. He searched the criminal quarters of the city where he lived and the prisons for one whose face should meet the requirements of his conception of Judas. At length he found in a cell in the prison a man who was condemned to death for murder. This was the face for which he was looking. From time to time he would visit the prison and work on the portrait. One day, when the portrait was finished, he took it to his studio and chanced to place it alongside the painting of Jesus as a child. Looking at the two portraits together, he thought that he discerned a certain similarity. So struck was he with the likeness that he went to the prison and looked up the record of the prisoner whose face he had painted. The search confirmed his opinion. The face of the child Jesus and the face of Judas were the face of the same man, in childhood and in manhood.

True or not, this story sets before us the possibilities, and the dread possibilities, of every human soul. One of the old commentators, when he came to the passage in John's Gospel which tells of the betrayal by Judas, sketched on the margin the face of a babe sleeping on his mother's breast, and underneath it wrote, "Judas!" John, in his account of the treason of Judas, makes this comment, "that the Scriptures might be fulfilled." And that raises at once the question of Judas and predestination. The Book of the Acts of the Apostles, in telling of the end of Judas, says that Judas "by his transgression fell, that he might go to his own place." Both verses raise the question of predestination, and whether or not Judas was chosen of old to play his dreadful part. What place had the son of perdition among the disciples of the Son of Man? Life has too much deep tragedy in it, too many instances of members of the same class or the same family, and objects of the same father's prayers and the same mother's love, who went, some to light and honor, and some, like Judas, to shame and infamy, out into the blackest night—for anyone to dismiss with a smile what God's Word tells us about the eternal decrees of heaven. Rossetti, in his *Jenny*, touches upon this mystery:

> Just as another woman sleeps!
> Enough to throw one's thoughts in heaps,
> Of doubt and horror—what to say.
> Or think—this awful secret sway,
> The potter's power over the clay!
> Of the same lump (it has been said)
> For honor and dishonor made two sister vessels;
> Here is one.

We can neither add to nor take from the words of Scripture

concerning this mystery of human faith and destiny; and there, in humble awe, we leave it. All that we can do is to speak of Judas on the side of his own will, his own decrees, and his own place. We cannot think, either, that he was chosen to play the part of traitor, as a stage manager might choose an actor to take the villain's part in a play; or that Judas joined the cause of Christ with purposes of treachery in his heart, or with unworthy mercenary motives. All the disciples hoped to gain something by their association with Christ; and near the very close of His ministry, Christ had to rebuke them for their worldly desires and ambitions.

What were his motives? Archbishop Whateley wrote a celebrated essay in which he tried to make out that Judas, disappointed that Jesus refused to let the people in Galilee make Him a king, resolved to force Jesus to take the messianic throne by bringing Him face to face with his adversaries, when He would be compelled to act. He therefore determined to betray Jesus, not in his heart, but for this worthy end, into the hands of His enemies at the time of the feast. But when Judas discovered how terrible a miscalculation he had made, and that Jesus had permitted Himself to be condemned to death, he hurried to the priests and made a last desperate effort to undo the sad business, and failing in this, overwhelmed with remorse and despair, he hanged himself. "The difference," says Archbishop Whateley, "between Iscariot and his fellow apostles was that though they had the same expectations and conjectures, he dared to act on his conjectures."

Thomas De Quincey, in his fantastic but entertaining essay on Judas, goes over much the same ground as Archbishop Whateley, only he exalts Judas to a far higher role than that assigned to him by the archbishop, who gives us a Judas who hoped to share in the glories of Christ's messianic reign. But the Judas of De Quincey's essay is a man of almost inconceivable self-sacrifice and lofty heroism. This Judas, knowing that the Scriptures must be fulfilled, and that Jesus must be betrayed into the hands of sinners before He will assert His royal power and take His messianic throne, resolves to play the role of traitor decreed from all eternity, fully conscious of the odium and infamy which will come to him. But when he saw that

Jesus permitted Himself to be put to death, his heart broke with remorse.

Unfortunately, this Judas of the archbishop and of De Quincey is a figment of pure imagination, such stuff as dreams are made of, and not the Judas of the New Testament. The only source that we have for knowledge about Judas tells us that he was a traitor who sold his Lord, not to fulfill the Scriptures, or force Jesus into the assumption of messianic claims, but for the sake of thirty pieces of silver. The fourth Evangelist and the Gospel of Luke speak of him with a shudder, saying, "Satan entered into him." If in the character of Judas we confront the mystery of predestination, here also we confront the darker mystery of the satanic element in human nature. Very likely Judas was just as sincere in his motives, as worthy or unworthy, as the rest of the disciples when he joined the Twelve. In the case of the other eleven, contact with Christ seems to have drawn out the good and banish the evil. With Judas, the reverse seems to have been the case. Avarice, undoubtedly, played its part in his downfall. John says plainly that he was a thief and stole from the treasury. This thieving instinct made him blow with his tainted breath upon the beautiful offering of Mary to Jesus, complaining that the money might have been given to the poor. Judas is perhaps the most successful of any of the portraits in Leonardo's great painting. There he sits with furtive brow and dark visage, clutching the bag with an eager right hand.

Judas was not the first victim of avarice. Men with visions of the truth, and with a store of good motives, have been brought to a disastrous end through the love of filthy lucre. Perhaps Jesus looked at Judas now and then, when He spoke those often repeated warnings about covetousness and laying up treasure in heaven. It is possible, too, that vindictiveness and revenge entered into his crime as well as avarice. Judas knew that Jesus knew from the beginning that he was a traitor, or, at least, had treasonable propensities. Once He said that one of His disciples had a devil. Perhaps He looked at Judas when He said that. It is significant that both Matthew and Mark say it was after Jesus had rebuked him for interfering with Mary's gift of precious ointment, that Judas began to seek opportunity to betray Him. The devil of vengeance began to brood in the heart of Judas. This helps me to understand that kiss in the Garden of Gethsemane. The leaders of the band must have known Jesus, and such a sign was hardly necessary. But to a vindictive, revengeful spirit, the darkest, cruelest spirit that can possess the soul of man or the heart of woman, how sweet that midnight kiss.

When Judas had received the sop, two things happened. Jesus said, "That thou doest, do quickly: then Satan entered into him." This marks the crisis in the soul of Judas. He chose evil rather than good; darkness rather than light. How significant, although perhaps accidental, is the comment of John. "He went immediately out, *and it was night.*" And what a night!

There have been worse men than Judas, perhaps, for there have been great sinners who seem to have had no remorse for their sins. Judas certainly had. The old commentators and preachers used to try to show the difference between what they called the repentance of Peter and the remorse of Judas. I know there must be a difference, and yet I confess I have never been able to see just what that difference was. Peter went out into the night and wept bitterly; Judas came back with the blood money, and, throwing it on the table before the priests and the Pharisees, cried, "I have sinned in that I have betrayed innocent blood." When he saw that his change of mind was too late to save Christ from condemnation and death, then he went out and hanged himself. There we begin to pity Judas. For that matter, every wrongdoer comes to the place where not only he himself, but men and angels must pity him. After all, like every sinner, Judas sold himself and went to his own place.

> Still as of old,
> Man by himself is priced;
> For thirty pieces, Judas sold himself,
> Not Christ.

COMPARISON

Balaam and Judas are the darkest shadows of the Old Testament and the New Testament, and their careers attract us and yet distract us. Each is a moral enigma which human wisdom cannot solve. In the galleries of Europe one can always pick out a portrait by the Toledo painter, El Greco, by the dark shading which that artist so often employed. These portraits of Balaam and Judas are both darkly shaded, shaded with the mystery of fate and predestination. They were both men who stood in the bright light of truth and divine revelation, and yet men who wandered off into the darkness.

Both Balaam and Judas were men of superior parts and opportunities. We know that Balaam, at least, was a genius, one of the most eloquent men of the Old Testament; and Judas must have had some capacity, else he would not have been chosen by Jesus Christ. In that sense, both represent the sad prostitution of great gifts. David lamented over Saul and Jonathan that they had fallen on Gilboa—"as though they had not been anointed with oil." So fell Balaam and Judas, both of them anointed with the oil of special calling and special guidance and inspiration, and yet dying as if they had not been anointed.

Both men went to their doom in spite of repeated warnings and remonstrances. Balaam had to rush greedily through the barrier of his own conscience and past the sword of the angel. Judas more than once was warned by Jesus. Yet both men insisted on going to their own place. Both men tampered with conscience. Their eye was not single and the light that was in them became darkness.

Both Balaam and Judas were slain by avarice. For gold, Balaam seduced Israel to sin, through the medium of the Moabitish women; and Judas for thirty pieces of silver betrayed Christ.

Both Judas and Balaam tell us that religious environment, high religious office, spiritual ambitions, spiritual language and religious desires are not in themselves sufficient to save a man from sin and judgment, unless he also sets himself to do the will of God. John Bunyan brings *Pilgrim's Progress* to a tragic conclusion by showing us a door to hell close to the gate of heaven, through which a careless pilgrim is thrust. So, close to the highest spiritual privileges and offices and desires, there may be a door which opens into hell.

Both Balaam and Judas were terrible and wretched in their death. What a picture is that!—the old prophet from the East, with his garments all stained with blood, and his eyes staring heavenward, as he lies there amid the heaps of Midianitish dead, fallen in battle against the God of Israel! And what a picture is this, too; this body swaying to and fro in the night wind—all that is left of the man who has gone "to his own place"!

6

ELIJAH AND JOHN THE BAPTIST

ELIJAH

Elijah and his prophecies are catapulted on the stage of history without prelude or introduction. All we are told is that Elijah the Tishbite, who was of the inhabitants of Gilead, stood before Ahab, king of Israel, and said, "As the Lord God of Israel liveth before whom I stand, there shall not be dew nor rain these years; but according to my word." Seed which is sown today does not come to the harvest today, but tomorrow. The apostasy of Jeroboam, who made Israel to sin, bore its evil harvest in the days of King Ahab, when the religion of Jehovah was proscribed and there was an altar to Baal on every high hill and under every green tree.

Elijah's prophecy was accompanied by prayer, and centuries afterward when he wished to show what prayer could do, James cites the example of Elijah, saying, "Elias was a man subject to like passions as we are, and he prayed earnestly that it might not rain; and it rained not on the earth by the space of three years and six months." If all there is to prayer is just the emotional reaction and effect it has upon those who pray, making us feel better and stronger, then prayer must be something else than what is called prayer in the Bible. There the effectual fervent prayer of righteous men avails much.

In his lonely retreat on the banks of the Brook Cherith the life of Elijah was miraculously preserved. He who cannot stand a miracle had better not take up the Bible, for it is nothing else than the story of God in action, one long miracle from the creation of the world to the creation of the new heavens and the new earth. Some think to make Christianity and the Bible more acceptable to men by stripping them of their one grand characteristic, the supernatural. So Rousseau, in Émile makes *The Vicar of Savoy* say that by taking the miracles out of the Bible, we will have the world at the feet of Jesus. He does not seem to see that the Jesus at whose feet the world would be bowing would be only a man.

Between Elijah's dramatic appearance at the court of Ahab, and the next great scene on Mount Carmel, there comes a pleasant interlude at the home of the widow of Zarephath. As Jesus was strengthened for His trial in Gethsemane and Golgotha by the two sisters of Bethany, so Elijah was prepared for Carmel by the widow of Zarephath. It is written that he that receives a prophet in the name of a prophet shall have a prophet's reward. The reward of this woman was not only the miraculous increase in her barrel of meal and cruse of oil, but the bringing to life of her dead son.

All this time Ahab had been hunting for Elijah, but instead of Ahab finding Elijah, it is Elijah who finds the king. When they meet, Ahab says to Elijah, "Art thou he that troubleth Israel?" Elijah answers: "I have not troubled Israel; but thou, and thy father's house, in that ye have forsaken the commandments of the Lord, and thou hast followed Baalim." Then came the trial by fire on the slopes of Carmel.

Carmel was a fit arena for such a contest. From its rugged slopes one could behold the whole panorama of Israel. To the east was Horeb and Seir, and far beyond, the plains of Arabia; to the south, Jericho and the Dead Sea. To the north, snow-crowned Hermon and Tabor. At the foot of Carmel lay the valley of Esdraelon, the battleground of nations, ancient and modern; while to the west rolled the Great Sea. In the presence of the king and all the people of Israel, two altars were built, one to Baal and one to Jehovah, and the sacrifices laid upon it. But no fire was kindled. That was to come from heaven. From dawn until noon, and from noon until the shadows were falling across the valley, the priests of Baal cried, "Oh, Baal, hear us." In their frenzy they leaped upon the altar and cut themselves with knives and lances until the blood gushed out upon them. But there was no voice, nor anyone that answered. These priests of Baal, bad servants of a false god, nevertheless could teach Christian disciples and followers of the true God some worthwhile lessons. They were willing to sacrifice for their faith, cutting themselves with knives. They persevered all through the day, even though no answer came; and they kept on praying in spite of the mockery and ridicule of Elijah. But their prayers were in vain because there was no Baal.

When they had ended their incantations, Elijah repaired a fallen altar of Jehovah, and having thoroughly drenched the sacrifice with water, so that there could be no doubt as to divine intervention, he lifted up his voice and prayed, saying, "Hear me, O Lord, hear me, that this people may know that Thou the Lord art God, and that Thou hast turned their hearts back." Then the fire of the Lord fell, and consumed the burnt offering and licked up the water that was in the trench. When the people saw it they fell on their faces, and said, "The Lord, He is God."

Elijah now announced to Ahab that rain was at hand. "Get thee up, eat and drink; for there is the sound of the abundance of rain." Only Elijah could hear that sound, and he heard it only with the ear of faith. Taking his servant with him, by tradition, the youth whose life he had restored, the son of the widow of Zarephath, Elijah ascended to the top of Carmel. There he prostrated himself in prayer, and said to his servant, "Go up now, look toward the sea." The young man climbed to the highest elevation, and looked off toward the west. But nowhere could he see what Elijah had sent him to see. Below lay the parched valleys, and beyond the glassy sea, its still, unruffled waters flaming like an opal as the sun sank into its depths. Not a breath of air was stirring, not a cloud appeared in all the expanse of the heavens, and not a single whitecap on the sea told of the approaching storm. He extended the palms of his hands, but they felt not a single drop of rain. He then went back to Elijah, and said, "There is nothing." Elijah, still prostrate in prayer, said to him, "Go again"; and again the youth climbed to the peak and scanned the horizon for the sign of rain, and again he returned to Elijah with his report, "There is nothing." This was repeated seven times. The seventh time, the young man saw a small cloud arising out of the sea. Going back to Elijah, he said, "Behold, there ariseth a cloud out of the sea as small as a man's hand." Elijah now knew that the answer to his prayer had come, and he sent his servant before him to tell Ahab to make ready his chariot and start for the capital, before the floods made the roads impassable. Before he himself had descended the mountain, the heavens grew black with clouds, the wind began to shake the cedars, the lightning began to play along the hills, the thunder rolled over land and sea, and there was a great rain.

Elijah's great faith had been mightily vindicated in the conflict with the priests of Baalim and Carmel, and then in the coming of rain after three years of drought. But it is only a step from Mount Carmel to the juniper tree, from the loftiest peak of exultation to the lowest valley of doubt and the driest desert of despair. "The lark which has sung her song at the very gate of heaven, sinks at last, wearied and voiceless, into the brown furrow. The height of the crest of one wave measures the depth of the trough of the next." The next time we see Elijah, he is lying beneath a juniper tree of the desert, asking God to take away his life. After his victory over the priests of Baal, Elijah, strong in his success, girded up his loins and ran before Ahab to the entrance of Jezreel. There his enthusiasm suddenly left him; for there met him a messenger from Jezebel threatening him with death on the morrow: "So let the gods do to me, and more also, if I take not thy life as the life of one of them by tomorrow about this time." As a prophet of Jehovah in the exercise of his duties and his commissions, Elijah was attended by the power and majesty of God; but as a man, he was alone, feeble, and helpless. He had to save his own life as any other man pursued by the wrath of a wicked queen. He arose and "went for his life," and came to Beersheba, at the extreme south of the country. There he left his servant and plunged into the wilderness another day's journey. In that same wilderness where Hagar and Ishmael had wandered in their exile, Elijah held his course until the blinding heat of the desert smote him to his knees and made him seek the shade of a lone juniper tree. Not even Hagar, weeping for her son, dying of thirst beneath the shrub, was more disconsolate and wretched than Elijah as he lay beneath the juniper tree, praying for the peace of death: "It is enough; now, O Lord, take away my life; for I am not better than my fathers."

Ministered to by the angel, Elijah now goes to Horeb, the mount of God. There he heard the Word of God, "What doest thou here, Elijah?" Elijah, in his reply, told of his jealousy for the Lord God of Hosts, and yet how the children of Israel had forsaken the covenant of God, thrown down His altars, slain His prophets with the sword, and he was the only worshiper of God left; and now his life, too, was in jeopardy. To cure Elijah of his despondency, and to show him the resources of the Almighty, God speaks to him by the still small Voice. Elijah knew much of God before he went into that desert; but there he learned more of God. He had known the God of majesty, the God of the thunder and the thick cloud; but now he was to learn something of God's love and gentleness, of the God who knew that Elijah was dust and remembered his frame. The rocks were rent with the wind; but God was not in the wind. The earth trembled; but God was not in the earthquake. The mountain burned with the fire; but God was not in the fire. Then after the fire, a still small Voice— "And it was so when Elijah heard it that he wrapped his face in his mantle and went out and stood in the entering in of the cave." Then again came the Voice, "What doest thou here, Elijah?" And again Elijah asserted his loyalty to God and his covenant, and lamented the general apostasy of Israel.

In dealing with His despondent prophet, God spoke no word of condemnation or rebuke. All that He did was to grant him a new commission for further service. He was to anoint Jehu, king over Israel; Hazael, king over Syria; and Elisha to be his own successor. Then He told him that his despondency was not warranted by the facts; that instead of there being just one loyal prophet and worshiper in Israel, there were seven thousand who had not bowed the knee to Baal. The best cure for Elijah was a summons to work for God. It was foolish presumption for Elijah to despair of the world, as if it were his world, and would fall to pieces the moment he ceased to support it. God very gently taught him this when He told him to anoint the unknown plowboy in his stead. John Keble used to say, "When you are quite despondent, the best way is to go out and do something kind to somebody." This is a medicine which never fails to cure.

Great in his life, Elijah was great in his sunset. Nothing in his life became him like the leaving of it. What a sunset it was! How tender this rugged prophet of denunciation and of judgment is, when he comes to take his farewell of Elisha. He said to Elisha, as if to spare him the pain of parting, "Tarry here, I pray thee, for the Lord has sent me to Bethel." But Elisha refused to leave his master, and went down with him to Bethel. From Bethel they went to the Jordan, where Elijah took his mantle and cleft with it a path through the waters. Then, when he had asked Elijah to make his last request, and Elisha had asked for a double portion of his master's spirit, behold, there appeared a chariot of fire and horses of fire and parted them both asunder. And Elijah went up by a whirlwind into heaven. Elisha, seeing this glorious transfiguration, and in it God's vindication of His great prophet, cried out, "My Father, my Father; the chariot of Israel, and the horsemen thereof!"

The epilogue to this great drama of Elijah's life is when he appeared in glory with Moses on the Mount of Transfiguration and spoke with Christ about His atonement. We all understand why Moses, through whom came the Law, which was a schoolmaster to bring men to Christ, was selected for that high distinction. But why Elijah? Why not Moses and Isaiah, the evangelical prophet? Or why not Moses and Abraham, through whom the first covenant was made? Or why not Moses and David, the royal type of David's son? But the record of the evangelist is not Moses and Isaiah, nor Jeremiah, nor David, nor Abraham; but Moses and Elijah. Elijah, in an age of apostasy and unbelief, courageously and heroically witnessed to God and proclaimed his faith to the world. It is impossible to overestimate the meaning to the world of such a man, and the everlasting symbol of that meaning and worth we read, when we see Elijah called out of the unseen world to stand with Moses and speak with Christ concerning the triumphant redemption which was to be finished on Calvary's Cross.

JOHN THE BAPTIST

Writing of the Baptist, one has said of him, "He keeps growing upon the imagination of mankind. His death casts a spell upon the heart. Because he lived, it is easier for us to hate weakness and cowardice and cruelty, and to imitate the humility and the heroism of this son of thunder. It is those who have suffered who come the nearest to us, and who inspire us most to climb the difficult and upward way."

When Wendell Phillips spoke over the mountain grave of John Brown, he said: "Men will believe more firmly in virtue now that such a man has lived and died." John is decisively that sort of a man. It was fitting that the Son of God should have a mighty forerunner. And what a forerunner John was, worthy of that high encomium which Jesus pronounced upon him, when He said that John was the greatest man that had ever lived; "Among them that are born of women there hath not arisen a greater than John the Baptist."

In the case of John the Baptist, the veil of childhood and ancestry is lifted for us a little and we are permitted to see something of the sources of this great river of power and influence. Writing of the Baptist, John the Evangelist said, "There was a man sent from God whose name was John." Back of all our histories and biographies and heredity and environment and education lies the mighty purpose of God.

But in sending great men into the world, God lets them come through channels and instrumentalities which sometimes lie within our observation. If John was the greatest man that ever lived, this is the first thing we want to know about him: Who was the father and who the mother of such a man? and who his grandfather? and who his grandmother? Luke, always the careful and explicit historian, lays great stress on that part of John's history which comes before his birth, "There was a certain priest named Zacharias of the course of Abia: and his wife was of the daughters of Aaron, and her name was Elisabeth; and they were both righteous before God."

Another element in John's preparation was his early training; first, in his home. The angel said of him, "He shall be great in the sight of the Lord and shall drink no wine nor strong drink from his mother's womb." Luxury and self-indulgence had no place in the training of this greatest of the sons of men. He who was to condemn the world was preeminently a man who showed the world that he could do without it. From the time that he was able to think and to discern between his left hand and his right hand, John was taught to deny himself. Then came his training in the wilderness. He was in the desert until the day of his showing to Israel. John's character was shaped in solitude. He retired from the face of man that he might more clearly see the face of God.

Brought into the world by a godly father and mother, and through the plan and purpose of the Almighty, schooled in solitude by self-denial, learning to endure hardness, John entered upon the arena of his great career. His preaching was the preaching of repentance and of judgment. He told of the advent of the Messiah and humbled himself before Him, saying, "He must increase; but I must decrease." As every true herald of Christ ought to be, John was the true friend of the Bridegroom. When the Bridegroom comes, this great friend begins to fade from the page of the Gospels, as fades the day star before the glorious beams of the sun.

But before he passed from the stage, John was permitted to hail and salute Him whose coming he had foretold. And with what a sentence did he salute Him! All the eternal purpose of God to redeem a race, all the long preparation through patriarch, prophet, sacrifice and law, and all the great meaning of Calvary, and all the rich music and chorus of the redeemed in heaven is summed up in that sentence of John, spoken at the Jordan, "Behold the Lamb of God which taketh away the sin of the world."

John's sun seemed to go down in darkness. In the lonely fortress of Machaerus, on the shores of the Dead Sea, John's eagle eye began to film and his mighty spirit began to flag. "Art Thou He that should come, or look we for another?" was the message of doubt that John sent to Jesus from the dungeon, by two of his disciples. To encourage him, Jesus sent him back this word: "Go and shew John again those things which you do hear and see: the blind receive their sight, the deaf hear, the lame walk, the lepers are cleansed, the dead are raised up, and the poor have the Gospel preached unto them." What effect this had upon John in his hour of trial, we know not. We like to think that before the night came down, there was light for him at eventide. John's death was the price he paid for his courageous denunciation of Herod and his adulterous union with Herodias. As far as Herod was concerned, John could have lived, for Herod frankly admired him and frequently had him discourse on the things pertaining to the kingdom of God. But the enmity of Herodias, trapping Herod through a clever device, the wanton dancing of the beautiful Salome, secured from the reluctant king what she desired, the head of John the Baptist.

COMPARISON

Elijah and John the Baptist have a certain similarity even in their outward appearance and dress. When Elijah had told the messengers of Ahaziah that his fall through a lattice in his chamber would prove fatal, the king asked them to describe the man who had met them by the way. They answered, "He was an hairy man and girt with a girdle of leather about his loins." That was enough for Ahaziah. The description told him that it was none other than the great Elijah. Of John the Baptist it is recorded by Mark, "And John was clothed with camel's hair, and with a girdle of a skin about his loins, and he did eat locusts and wild honey."

Elijah and John were both children of solitude and meditation. Solitude is the mother country of strong souls. Both Elijah and John the Baptist were graduates, magna cum laude, of the University of the Desert.

Both Elijah and John the Baptist were given messages of judgment and denunciation, and in the discharge of their commission both displayed superb courage. Elijah denouncing Ahab and Jezebel, and John the Baptist calling the scribes and the Pharisees a generation of vipers, and telling Herod that it was not lawful for him to have his brother's wife for his own. Both preached personal, intimate sermons of condemnation for great sins, as Nathan once denounced David, saying to him, "Thou art the man!"

Both men were pursued by the enmity of a wicked woman, than which there is nothing fiercer or more terrible out of hell or in it. Because he had slain the prophets of Baal, her pampered pets, Jezebel vowed that Elijah's head should not stand upon his shoulders; and Herodias, through the sensuous dancing of her daughter, Salome, won from Herod the fatal concession, the head of John the Baptist. Elijah, through the providence of God, escaped the murderous wrath and the fury of Jezebel and had a glorious translation to heaven. John, by the providence of God, was shut up in a prison and his head brought in on a silver charger to add merriment to a banquet.

Both men, great and sublime in their faith, suffered a temporary eclipse and passed under the cloud of doubt. Elijah, after his triumph on Mount Carmel, fell on his face beneath the juniper tree, and asked God to take away his life, telling Him that he was no better than his fathers; that is, that he could do no more than the previous generations in stemming the tide of popular iniquity. John the Baptist, when he had been shut up in the dungeon, and Jesus did not intervene to get him out, and showed no flashing of the ax of judgment, which John had said He would lay to the roots of the tree of evil, began to doubt if Jesus was the Messiah, and said to Him, "Art Thou He that should come, or look we for another?" Like other great and heroic souls after them—Luther, John Knox, Cromwell—both Elijah and John the Baptist recoiled for a moment from before that vast, huge rampart of the world's unbelief and sin, to human thought at times so invincible and unscalable, and before whose walls so many hosts in the past have perished. Both were lifted out of the pit of their despondency by learning what God was doing, and what He would yet do. God told Elijah of seven thousand who had not bowed the knee to Baal, and gave him a commission to carry on his work through an unknown and hitherto unnamed successor, Elisha. Christ told John the Baptist that he could trust in Him as the Messiah because the blind were seeing, the deaf hearing, the lame walking and the dead being raised up.

Both men are immortal in their influence. Elijah, or John the Baptist—either name is like an army with banners; and their mighty accents still speak like voices in the wilderness.

Elijah's highest reward and vindication, and the chief proof of the greatness of his influence, was his appearance with Moses on the Mount of Transfiguration when he spoke with Christ concerning His decease which He should accomplish at Jerusalem. The highest tribute paid to John's posthumous greatness was what Herod said when he heard of the miracles of Jesus, "John, whom I beheaded, is risen from the dead."

The Old Testament comes to a conclusion with a prediction of the coming again of Elijah, "Behold, I will send you Elijah the prophet before the coming of the great and dreadful day of the Lord: And he shall turn the heart of the fathers to the children, and the heart of the children to their fathers, lest I come and smite the earth with a curse." When the angel told Zacharias that a child whose name should be John was to be born to him and Elisabeth, he said of him, "And he shall go before Him in the spirit and power of Elias, to turn the hearts of the fathers to the children, and the disobedient to the wisdom of the just; to make ready a people prepared for the Lord." That is always what we are thinking about as we follow the story of John the Baptist in the Gospels. Always by his side stands the great prophet of the days of Ahab and Jezebel. How like John is to Elijah, we are always saying to ourselves. This impression is confirmed and vindicated by what Jesus said when He came down from the Mount of Transfiguration. The disciples had asked Jesus, "Why, then, say the Scribes that Elijah must first come?" referring to the last echo of prophecy in the last verse of the last book of the Old Testament. Jesus answered, "Elias truly shall first come, and restore all things. But I say unto you, That Elias is come already, and they knew him not, but have done unto him whatsoever they listed. Likewise shall also the Son of man suffer of them. Then the disciples understood that He spake unto them of John the Baptist."

7

SAMUEL AND BARNABAS

SAMUEL

When Saul asked the witch of Endor to bring up Samuel, and the woman, evidently surprised at the apparition of Samuel, cried out with a loud voice, Saul asked her what she saw. The woman answered, "I see a god coming up out of the earth." Then Saul, perceiving it was Samuel, fell on his face on the ground. Samuel was godlike even in his death. That is the way he impresses us wherever we come upon him in the drama of Israel's history. He was not only a godly, but a godlike man. There is a majesty in his life which makes him rise out of the mists of antiquity like a god.

Life is a book of three volumes. A great number never get past the first volume. A still larger number never go beyond the second volume. And to only a few is it permitted to live and write the third and final volume. In the life of Samuel no volume is wanting, and each volume has its full quota of chapters. There are not many men in the Bible whom we can follow from the cradle to the grave. Some begin in youth and end in middle life; or they appear in middle life, and pass from the stage in old age. Even where we do commence with a man at his birth and end with his death and burial, there are long and meaningless blanks in his biography. Samuel, on the contrary, is an open book from beginning to end. We hear the prayers which were

69

uttered before he was born, and we are amazed at the influence of his life after he is dead.

Samuel did not stumble upon greatness. When it comes to seers, prophets, and godlike men, we find that there has been a preparation for their lives before they were born. If Samuel was a godlike man, let us not forget that scene in the House of the Lord, where the sorrowing mother, kneeling in the silent temple, entreated God for a child. Shaftesbury once said, "Give me a generation of Christian mothers, and I will undertake to change the basis of society in twelve months." When we try to measure the godlike Samuel, we must not forget his mother of faith and prayer. Men do not gather grapes of thorns, nor figs of thistles; neither do great men of God come from worldly and irreligious mothers.

Samuel qualified for his career as a prophet by uncompromising loyalty to the truth at the very threshold of his public life. The youth naturally feared to tell Eli what he had learned in the vision, how judgment was to fall upon Eli and his whole house. That was Samuel's first temptation. Would he tell Eli half the truth? tone down the message? take the sting out of it? Just as the smallest stone determines whether the mountain stream shall flow east or west, to the Gulf and the Atlantic, or to the Pacific, so there are turning points in the moral history of every life. Samuel told Eli every whit and hid nothing from him. Henceforth, he is always the man who declares all that God has commanded him. Whether dealing with the corrupt nation or wayward Saul, or the youthful David, or appearing again on earth out of the world of spirits, Samuel is the man who tells every whit and hides nothing. He has the ring of sincerity and truth about him.

There are two kinds of authority in the world, that which rests upon force, and that which rests upon character. That which rests upon force can be quickly destroyed; a revolution, a floating mine, a stick of dynamite, a bullet, or a dagger overthrows it. That which rests upon character is as unassailable and eternal as the hills. Samuel had the authority of character. The last of the judges and the first of the prophets, he came to his office in a day of apostasy and degeneracy. Religion had fallen into the hands of vicious men. Shiloh was forsaken; the ark of God was taken; Ichabod was written over the face of the nation. Yet it was in that corrupt and adulterous generation that Samuel wielded the scepter of absolute moral and spiritual power. At Mizpeh he reconsecrated the people and led a nation back to God.

The last trial of Samuel was the hardest. How will this man, who has wielded undisputed authority and influence, now face the winds of adversity? The real test is how a man looks when the sun has gone down on him; when adulation, flattery, and its fickle crowd are gone, and the man stands alone, wrapped in the mists for a mantle, with the darkness coming down upon him? Here, if ever, we see Samuel as a god coming up out of that darkness.

In consideration of what he had done for the nation, the people might have overlooked his old age and the misdeeds of his unworthy sons, for this godlike man had to bear the cross of godless sons. But gratitude is not one of the natural graces of mankind. Like a blow in the face came the cruel and abrupt demand of the people—"Behold thou art old; and thy sons walk not in thy ways. Now make us a king to judge us like all the nations." It was one of those moments when ghostlike interrogation marks suddenly rise to stand with mockery and menace after all we have held to be true and abiding. Was it worthwhile to serve others? Was it worthwhile to live well? Or have I been infatuated with a shadow? Have I pursued a phantom? Feelings like these, I suppose, swept over the soul of this man of God. Yet in that hour he did nothing mean or common; no angry retort, no peevish lamentation; but childlike submission, when it is made clear to him that God will act through this request of the people for a king. The heart of the rejected old Samuel, his head grey, his back with years bent, is the same heart of the child who in the House of the Lord, before the Lamp had gone out, answered when he heard the voice, "Speak, Lord, for Thy servant heareth." God told Samuel that in asking for a king they had rejected God, and not Samuel. "They have not rejected thee, but Me." When a man identifies himself with the plan of God and with the truth of God, his work never fails. The new order comes in and the old prophet bows to it. Rejected of Israel, he will yet remember Israel at the altar of prayer. "As for me," he said, "God forbid that I should sin against the Lord in ceasing to pray for you." Samuel took his revenge upon Israel for their rejection of him by praying for them. A fine revenge, too, that is, to take upon those who have hurt us, or wounded us, or wronged us, to pray for them as Samuel prayed for Israel.

Tall in his life, Samuel seems even taller in his death. In that great scene from the Old Testament, we behold Saul, or the wreck of Saul, pale and haggard, leaning upon his sword upon Mount Gilboa's slopes. Below him is encamped the vast army of the Philistines. Saul was a real soldier, and not easily frightened; but the hum of this mighty army filled him with misgivings. In this hour of danger and hovering judgment, Saul reached out for a help greater than his own. The oracles were dumb; God answered him not; no vision came on the wings of a dream; no mystic light flashed from the stones on the breastplate of the High Priest; none from the schools of the prophets could answer him. In his despair he knocks on the door of the underworld. When the witch of Endor asks him, "Whom shall I bring up to thee?" Saul does not hesitate for a moment. Not Abraham, Moses, Joshua, Gideon, nor any other of the great men of the past, does he ask for; but Samuel. It is as if he had said, "Bring up Samuel! I mocked at his counsels. I grieved his heart. I disregarded his warnings. But now the night is dark, and I am far from home. Call up the man who anointed me king and kissed my brow before I was defiled with sin. Call up the man of God who never feared to speak the truth for me. Call up the man who went down to his grave mourning for me and praying for me. If any man, living or dead, can help me or save me now, it is he. Call up Samuel!" That was one of the greatest tributes ever paid to a good man. Good men never die. They rest from their labors; their works do follow them. Samuel was dead, but his influence is alive forevermore. He died and disappeared as a man; but he came back as one of the gods.

BARNABAS

With a man like St. Paul the chief actor on the New Testament stage, other men are at a great handicap. The light of their life seems dim and feeble in comparison with the bright and burning star, St. Paul. But there were great men before Paul; and great men, too, at his side. One of them was Barnabas. This was not his first and family name, which was Joseph. But after he became a Christian at Jerusalem, the apostles called him Barnabas, the son of consolation and exhortation. Probably "exhortation" or "prophecy" is a better rendering than "consolation." But the Christian church generally has adopted the interpretation, "the son of consolation"; and homes of St. Barnabas, where the sick and helpless are cared for, are found all over the world; and beautiful monuments, too, to the life and influence of Barnabas.

Barnabas was a native of the island of Cyprus; a Levite, and evidently of a family of standing and property, for we are told that Barnabas having land sold it and brought the money and laid it at the apostle's feet. As Tarsus was not far from Cyprus, the home of Barnabas, it is barely possible that he was acquainted with Paul and his family. At all events, when Paul was converted and, having escaped death at Damascus, came to Jerusalem and tried to join the disciples, they were all afraid of him and believed not that he was a disciple. But Barnabas took him and brought him to the apostles, and declared unto them how he had seen the Lord on the way, and that he had spoken to Him, and how he had preached boldly at Damascus in the name of Jesus. After Paul's bloody record as a persecutor of Christianity, it required almost another miracle to secure him standing in the Christian church. No one would trust him or accept him. Barnabas was the man of great faith who believed that the work of grace in Saul's heart was genuine, and it was he who vouched for him to the apostles at Jerusalem and persuaded them to dismiss their prejudice and receive him as a brother. If Barnabas had never done anything else than to speak for Paul at Jerusalem and introduce him to his work at Antioch, the world would still be his debtor. After Barnabas spoke for Paul, Peter took him into his own house, and that meant that Saul's battle for recognition was won.

The persecution that arose at the time of Stephen's death scattered Christian believers as far as Antioch and Cyprus, where they preached at first to Jews only. But at Antioch, a great number of the Grecians were converted. When news of this preaching came to the church at Jerusalem, Barnabas, who himself was a Greek-speaking Jew, and probably acquainted at Antioch, was sent down to take charge of the work there. When he arrived upon the scene he at once recognized the grave importance of what was taking place, and feeling the need of a helper, one better equipped to meet the situation than he was, he went down to Tarsus, where he found Paul and brought him back with him to Antioch. There the two men labored for a whole year. Thence it was that Paul and Barnabas, accompanied by the nephew of Barnabas, John Mark, sailed on the history-making voyage to Cyprus and Asia Minor.

Barnabas next appears with Paul as an advocate for Christian liberty before the Council of the church at Jerusalem, pleading for the rights of the Gentile Christians. When the decree of the Council had been delivered, asking that the Gentile Christians should abstain from idolatry, fornication, and from eating strangled animals and blood, it was delivered to the church at Antioch by Judas and Silas, together with Barnabas and Paul, "men that have hazarded their lives for the name of the Lord Jesus."

Having won this great battle for religious freedom and the expansion of the gospel, Paul and Barnabas (for the order has now changed from "Barnabas and Paul" to "Paul and Barnabas") plan to start from Antioch on a second missionary journey. Barnabas wished to take his nephew, Mark, again; but Paul, displeased with Mark because on the first missionary journey he had turned back when they reached Perga, would not consent to his going. Barnabas insisted on taking him, and thus came the separation between these two great men who had done so much for one another and for Christ. Barnabas went with Mark to Cyprus, and Paul and Silas traveled by the northern route which led them through Asia Minor into Europe. It is probable that this separation over John Mark was the climax to a difference between Paul and Barnabas in dealing with the Gentile Christians, for Paul tells us in his letter to the Galatians, how he rebuked Peter for his inconsistent course in eating with Gentile Christians at Antioch, and then refusing to eat with them when "certain from James" had come down to the city. Then he adds that even Barnabas "was carried away by their dissimulation." Perhaps, then, back of this dispute over John Mark there was a deeper difference as to the rights of the Gentile Christians.

After this separation from Paul, Barnabas passes from the stage of the New Testament history, save for an occasional mention by Paul in his letters, twice in the letter to the Galatians, once in the first letter to the Corinthians, and once in the letter to the Colossians. These references would indicate that the breach between them was healed. Tradition makes Barnabas a martyr at Salamis on the Island of Cyprus. When he was dying, according to the tradition, he told Mark to go back and join Paul.

COMPARISON

Samuel and Barnabas, like most of the great men of the Old and the New Testament, make their appearance at critical periods in the history of Israel and in the history of the church, Samuel in an age of idolatry and apostasy, when Israel is changing from its tribal condition to a monarchy; and Barnabas when the Christian church is changing from a Jewish sect to a world-conquering faith.

Both introduce great men to their work. Samuel anoints Saul, and when Saul has failed, he anoints David to be king over Israel. Barnabas wins recognition for Paul in the church at Jerusalem, and then launches him on his great missionary career at Antioch. They are both great men, for they are both acting at the springs of great energy and power.

Both are great in their devotion to the cause of God, and in their willingness to sink themselves for the sake of that cause. When Israel rejects Samuel and asks for a king, Samuel submits without a complaint and promises the people that he will still exercise for them the great office of intercession. Barnabas shows no resentment or jealousy, but rather a magnanimous generosity, when the fame of Paul eclipses his own fame and the record changes from Barnabas and Paul to Paul and Barnabas.

Both were sons of consolation and of prophecy. Samuel is the refuge of Israel in the time of trouble, and if to Saul, and sometimes to Israel, he must speak the words of judgment, he does so with the accents of sorrow and affection. Barnabas, who had won that name by the generous and charitable deeds at Jerusalem and elsewhere, proved himself the son of consolation and encouragement to the distrusted and suspicioned Paul. That is enough to make the church remember him forever.

Both men appear before us almost without a flaw or a blemish. The only shadow of rebuke which falls upon Samuel is when God remonstrates with him for his too great sorrow over Saul; and the only shadow of fault which falls over the character of Barnabas is his contention with Paul over John Mark. When we consider that John Mark was his nephew, and that Barnabas probably was anxious to have the young man redeem himself, as, indeed, he afterward did, it will be seen that this failing of Barnabas, like that of Samuel in the case of his grief over Saul, leans to virtue's side.

Both men lifted the thoughts of their fellowmen heavenward. Both were taken for gods. When the witch of Endor was asked by Saul to describe what she saw coming up out of the depths, she answered: "I see a god coming up out of the earth." When Paul had healed a lame man at Lystra, the people took them both, Barnabas and Paul, to be gods come down in the likeness of men. Because Paul did most of the speaking, they thought him to be Mercury; but Barnabas, with his noble and godlike presence, they called Jupiter.

8

ABEL AND STEPHEN

ABEL

One of the finest things in English poetry is that passage in Byron's *Cain*, where he describes Cain standing over the body of the murdered Abel, astonished at death, then new in the world, and now so old. The old, old fashion, and yet something which comes with new wonder and shock to the men of each new generation. Death in some other city, or in some other house down the street, is one thing; but when death invades our own house and family, we are forced to look on it with the same awe and surprise and wonder which Byron so splendidly imagines in the mind of Cain:

> Who makes me brotherless?
> His eyes are open! then he is not dead!
> Death is like sleep; and sleep shuts down our lids.
> His lips, too, are apart; why, then he breathes!
> And yet I feel it not. His heart!—his heart!
> Let me see, doth it beat? methinks—No!—
> This is a vision, else I am become
> The native of another and a worse world.
>
> But he cannot be dead!—Is silence death?
> No; he will wake: then let me watch by him.
> Life cannot be so slight as to be quenched

"

> Thus quickly!—He hath spoken to me since—
> What shall I say to him? My brother!—No;
> He will not answer to that name, for brethren
> Smite not each other. Yet—yet speak to me!
> Oh, for a word more of that gentle voice,
> That I may bear to hear my own again!"

The history of Abel and Cain introduces us to the first altar, the first murder, and the first death. Centuries after, James wrote, "Sin, when it is finished, bringeth forth death." Not until Cain slew his brother Abel were the wages of sin advertised to the world.

According to an old Muslim legend, the death of Abel was at the direct instigation of Satan. Cain, according to this story, was filled with envy and hatred toward his brother, but did not know how he could destroy his life. "But one day Satan placed himself in Cain's way as he walked with Abel in the fields, and seizing a stone, shattered therewith the head of an approaching wolf. Cain followed his example, and with a large stone struck his brother's forehead until he fell lifeless to the ground."

The altar can be traced clear back to the beginnings of the human race. The first literary records that we have of any people are always the records of their religion. Some think that today the altar has passed, and that worship is vanishing. Probably not; for the altar from the very beginning of the race has been linked with the history of mankind. The roots of the tree of human history are religious, and the final fruits of this tree will be religious. Human history, and the history of redemption, stretches from this first altar, where Cain and Abel sacrificed, to the altar and throne of the Lamb described in the Apocalypse about which shall gather the redeemed humanity.

The record in Genesis is that the Lord had respect to Abel and his offering; but to Cain and his offering, He had not respect. This difference can hardly have been in what was offered. Cain was a farmer and brought of the fruits of the soil. Abel was a shepherd and brought of the firstlings of his flock. Each brought what was proper and natural for him. The difference must have been, not in the offering, but in the men who made the offering. John tells us in his first letter that Cain slew his brother because his own works were evil and his brother's righteous. Abel comes down to history with the adjective "righteous" attached to his name, and that by the authority of our Lord Himself, who told the scribes and the Pharisees that they had shed righteous blood on the earth from the blood of righteous Abel to the blood of Zacharias, the son of Barachias. In just what particular this difference in character showed itself we cannot tell. But evidently, here, at the very beginning, we have that mysterious difference in character which we mark in men today. In the larger sense, there is none righteous; as the Bible tells us, "none that doeth good, no, not one." Yet, as between men and men, there is a great difference, and righteous Abel and righteous Job, and righteous Enoch, and men like them, stand out against the dark background of the world's evil.

The writer of the letter to the Hebrews makes the acceptable thing in the sacrifice of Abel the fact that it was offered by faith: "By faith Abel offered unto God a more excellent sacrifice than Cain; by which he obtained witness that he was righteous, God testifying of his gifts; and by it he being dead, yet speaketh." Abel appears as the first name in that grand roll call of the heroes who overcame through faith. Faith made a difference then, at the very fountain of human history; and faith makes a difference today. Christ said to the woman who was a sinner, "Thy sins are forgiven. Go in peace. Thy faith hath saved thee." Christ died between two thieves, an impenitent thief and a penitent thief. The difference between those two men and their destinies was the difference of faith. So Christ and His cross divide mankind into two groups—those who have faith, and those who do not.

God said to Cain, "What hast thou done? The voice of thy brother's blood crieth unto Me from the ground." Then He pronounced upon Cain the judgment of flight and vagabondage, and the struggle with a hostile soil for a living. Evil strikes its cruel and desperate blow and is answered at once by the judgment of God. The blood of Abel called to God for vengeance and justice. That blood, crimsoning for the first time the as yet unstained breast of the earth, spoke with fearful eloquence of the cruelty and atrocious nature of sin. Every drop of that blood which Cain now cannot gather up again speaks of the history of sin.

The blood of Abel spoke of judgment and retribution. The moment Abel's blood was shed it began to cry from the ground to God. Instantly, mysterious, divine forces are set in operation to repair the injury done to the divine order. The principles and conditions of the curse pronounced upon Cain's parents when they were driven out of Eden are reproduced in his own case. The earth, violated and profaned by the blood which he has shed, will refuse to yield him her fruit, and he himself is to be driven out from his home, a vagabond and a fugitive. No matter where Cain goes, Nod or elsewhere, or what great cities he may build (for he was the first builder of cities), or what new sons he brings into the world, he will never be able to forget that last look, that appealing cry, that strange, awful silence when he shed the blood of Abel. The blood of Abel speaks a fact that is just as true and as terrible today as on that fatal morning when Cain slew his brother— the fact of conscience and the fact of judgment.

In contrast with the cry for justice from the blood of Abel, is the cry for mercy from the blood of Christ. The author of the letter to the Hebrews speaks of Christ and His atonement as the "blood of sprinkling that speaketh better things than the blood of Abel." As the one spoke of retribution, so the other speaks of atonement, expiation and forgiveness. But we must remember that both are divine laws—God's justice and God's mercy. What makes it possible for sin to be forgiven is the death of Christ on the cross. There the judgment and the mercy, the holiness and the love of God, meet together. The blood of Abel spoke of hate, of man's inhumanity to man. The blood of Christ speaks of love, of love that one day shall bind and conquer all men in one family of faith and fellowship. We must never forget that when man kills man, it is one brother killing another, for God has made of one blood all nations of men to dwell on the face of the earth. When that oneness of humanity has been realized in a more vivid and powerful way than we now realize the *differences* of speech and race and custom, then men shall beat their swords into plowshares and their spears into pruning hooks.

STEPHEN

The old commentators used to see in Stephen's name, which is Greek for "crown," a prophecy of how he was to secure the martyr's crown. The story of his death introduces us to what the *Te Deum* so magnificently calls "the noble army of the martyrs."

Stephen was one of the seven deacons appointed by the church at Jerusalem to administer the charities and relieve the apostles of that burden. He is described as a man full of faith and grace and wisdom and the Holy Spirit. He speedily showed himself qualified for a greater work than that of the almoner of the church's charities. In the name of Christ he worked great miracles among the people, and in the synagogues of the Greek-speaking Jews he eloquently and powerfully defended the Christian faith.

Stephen now emerges as almost the chief figure in the church, the worker of miracles, the proclaimer of the gospel; and, at the end, the first martyr. All the apostles, even great Peter and John, seem to be in the background. He bridges the gap between the church as a Jewish institution and the church of the world, for it was directly through the persecution which arose at the time of his death that the Christian disciples, driven out of Jerusalem, went everywhere preaching the gospel; and, as we shall see, the death of Stephen and the conversion of Paul are very closely related.

When he was haled before the Sanhedrin, suborned witnesses, as in the case of Jesus, testified that they had heard him speak blasphemous words against Moses, against the temple, and against the law, saying that Jesus would destroy this place and change the customs of Moses. Arraigned before the Council, Stephen impressed everyone with his heavenly and radiant look. All they that sat in the Council saw his face as it had been the face of an angel. The heavenly light in his face that day was to be reflected in succeeding ages in the face of many a martyr as he stood undaunted at the stake, or in the Coliseum, or lay stretched on the rack.

In his poem, *The Two Voices*, Tennyson makes fine use of this incident of the angel look in Stephen's face:

> He heeded not reviling tones,
> Nor sold his heart to idle moans,
> Tho' cursed and scorn'd, and bruised with stones;
>
> But looking upward, full of grace,
> He prayed, and from a happy place
> God's glory smote him on the face.

At first, we do not see the connection between Stephen's long résumé of Hebrew history and the explosive and denunciatory conclusion of his apology. But we must remember that they had charged Stephen with careless words against the holy place. Although Stephen himself does not directly make the connection, when he speaks of how Abraham and Moses and David worshiped God, the clear inference is that the true worship is not to be confined to any one place, and that men can worship God anywhere in spirit and in truth. He had been charged, too, with speaking against Moses; but his answer is that Moses himself was rejected by the Jews, and that Moses predicted that God would raise up a great prophet in the future. Stephen believes that that Prophet was Christ, and that to follow Christ was not to repudiate Moses, but to obey him.

Stephen's speech comes to a conclusion with a volcanic eruption of judgment and denunciation, in which he demands of those who are trying him, and who, he well knows, will vote for his death as they had voted for the death of Jesus, "Which of the prophets have not your fathers persecuted? And they have slain them which showed before of the coming of the Just One, of whom ye have now been the betrayers and the murderers."

When they heard these things, the Jews in a wild fury rushed upon Stephen and dragged him out of the city to the place of execution, where they stoned Stephen as he called upon God. We think of a mob pressing upon Stephen and a shower of rocks battering him into a senseless mass. But the judgment of stoning to death was carefully carried out according to the tradition and custom of the Jews. This involved the procession to the place of punishment with the convicted man's crime on a placard, the compelling of the victim to kneel down and pray, the throwing of him from a height, and then the casting of two great stones on his body by the witnesses. The witnesses first of all must do the stoning, for they were the ones upon whose testimony the man had been convicted. When they had cast their stones, it made it safe for others to take a hand. So we have the picture here in the Acts of the witnesses against Stephen laying their garments for safekeeping at the feet of the young man named Saul. This orderly procedure will explain to us, too, how it was that Stephen had time to kneel down and pray.

In his death Stephen is the close disciple and imitator of his Lord and Master. When Jesus was crucified He prayed for His murderers, "Father, forgive them, for they know not what they do"; and when He was dying He prayed, "Into Thy hands I commend my spirit." When Stephen was stoned, he prayed for his murderers, "Lord, lay not this sin to their charge," and with his last breath, added, "Lord Jesus, receive my spirit." Those words, and also his prayer for them that did the wrong, have been repeated by many a martyr since as he marched to his fearful doom and yet glorious victory. It was the opinion of St. Augustine, and of Martin Luther, too, that it was this dying prayer of Stephen for his murderers which God used as the means for the conversion of the young man named Saul. If so, never did a greater prayer have a greater answer.

When a mere lad, Joseph Parker, the great English preacher, used to debate with infidels outside the Tyneside works. One day, an infidel asked him, "What did God do for Stephen?" the inference being that if there was a God, He certainly would have delivered His faithful witness out of the hand of his enemies. Parker answered—and he always felt that his answer was given him in that same hour of God, according to Christ's promise—"What did God do for Stephen? He gave him the power to pray for the forgiveness of those who stoned him."

One of the greatest things in this great picture of the death of the first martyr is the account of how Stephen, looking up into heaven, saw the glory of God and said, "Behold, I see the heavens open and Jesus standing on the right hand of God." To all succeeding ages this will ever be the picture and the symbol and the unbreakable promise of the Lord Jesus Christ, standing ready to intercede, to defend and to receive those

who are faithful in their witness to Him. These are the words
which John Keble takes as the starting point for his noble
poem, *St. Stephen's Day.*

> Foremost and nearest to His throne,
> By perfect robes of triumph known,
> And likest Him in look and tone
>   The holy Stephen kneels,
> With steadfast gaze, as when the sky
> Flew open to his fainting eye,
> Which like a fading lamp flash'd high,
>   Seeing what death conceals.
>
> Well might you guess what vision bright
> Was present to his raptured sight,
> Even as reflected streams of light
>   Their solar source betray—
> The glory which our God surrounds,
> The Son of Man, th' atoning wounds—
> He sees them all; and earth's dull bounds
>   Are melting fast away.
>
> He sees them all—no other view
> Could stamp the Savior's likeness true,
> Or with His love so deep embrue
>   Man's sullen heart and gross—
> "Jesu, do Thou my soul receive:
> "Jesu, do Thou my foes forgive:"
> He who would learn that prayer, must live
>   Under the holy Cross.
>
> He, though he seem on earth to move,
> Must glide in air like gentle dove,
> From yon unclouded depths above
>   Must draw his purer breath;
> Till men behold his angel face
> All radiant with celestial grace,
> Martyr all o'er, and meet to trace
>   The lines of Jesus' death.

COMPARISON

Abel was the first victim of sin. Stephen was the first victim of unbelief in Christ. Abel was the first martyr to righteousness. Stephen was the first martyr and witness to faith.

Both Abel and Stephen will stand forever as types of righteousness in an adulterous and sinful generation. Their deaths show what sin is and what sin will do.

Both men in their death show that evil is not unmarked by God, and that He knows how to avenge His saints. As soon as the blood of Abel was shed, it began to call from the ground for vengeance, and as soon as it called, God answered. While the stones were hurtling through the air, Stephen looked up into heaven and saw his Lord and Master standing at the right hand of God.

Both are heroes of faith. In the grand roll call of the eleventh chapter of the letter to the Hebrews, Abel's name comes first, "By faith, Abel." Were it permitted to us to add to that chapter, what a glorious addendum could be made; and brightest and fairest and most memorable among the names to be added would be the name of Stephen—

> The martyr first whose eagle eye,
> Could pierce beyond the grave,
> Who saw his Master in the sky
> And called on Him to save.

The blood of Abel calls for vengeance, proclaims the great law of God against sin. The blood of Stephen calls for vengeance, but the vengeance of forgiveness, the vengeance of light over darkness, of love over hate.

When Abel fell before the angry blow of Cain, death came into the world with all its terrors and with all its sting. But when Stephen fell beneath the stones of his murderers, death has been conquered by Christian faith; and so the sacred chronicler finishes, for this world, the history of Stephen by giving death a new name—"and when he had said this he fell asleep."

Both righteous Abel and faithful Stephen have long ago joined the heavenly chorus. Now Abel, whose blood once called for vengeance, sings a new song; and in that song he is joined by the first of the noble army of the martyrs, whose blood, of all that glorious host, first sealed a believer's witness to Christ. But now both martyrs and both singers forget their own blood, and how it was shed, as they gather about the throne of God and of the Lamb, and sing their praises to Him who had washed them—and can wash us all—from their sins by His own blood.

9

EBEDMELECH AND ONESIPHORUS

When Jesus said to His disciples in the desert of Caesarea Philippi, "Whom do men say that I the Son of man am?" they answered, "Some say that Thou art John the Baptist; some, Elias; and others, Jeremias." Both John and Elijah had Christ's flaming zeal and courageous denunciation of public iniquity and private sin. But neither was like Him in His pity, His tenderness, and His compassion. That we find in Jeremiah. He is the Old Testament's Man of Sorrows: and yet, at the same time, a brazen wall and a pillar of iron. The spell that he cast over Israel in succeeding generations is brought out in the legend that at a critical time in one of the battles for Israel's freedom, the prophet Jeremiah appeared and placed in the hand of Judas Maccabaeus a great sword with which he conquered his enemies.

No man ever had a more difficult commission than Jeremiah. In the day when the army of Babylon was at the gates of Jerusalem, it was his unpopular duty to counsel submission, declaring that the king of Babylon would certainly take and destroy the city. This made him the object of bitter hatred on the part of jealous nationalists and patriots. Nor was this strange. Unless they took him to be a prophet, speaking for God, and uttering words not his own, it was only natural that they should have resented his predictions. On one occasion, when Jeremiah was leaving the city to go to a town in the tribe of Benjamin, he was arrested by the Jewish army and charged with attempting to desert to the enemy. Zedekiah was then the weak king of Israel. He respected and feared Jeremiah as a prophet of the Lord. Yet he permitted him to be cast into a loathsome dungeon. He stoutly denied the charge that he was falling away to the Chaldeans; but the circumstances made his enemies suspicious, and he remained in the dungeon many days. Zedekiah then came to him and released him, and taking him secretly into the palace said, "Is there any word from the Lord?" If Jeremiah had been a false prophet, he might have made some optimistic prediction and thus escaped from prison. But he was faithful to his message, and said to the king, "There is: for thou shalt be delivered into the hands of the king of Babylon." In answer to Jeremiah's entreaty that he be not recommitted to the dungeon in the house of Jonathan, Zedekiah let him remain in the court of the prison, evidently a less cruel and rigorous confinement.

But the princes and leaders of Jerusalem, angered at the prophecies of Jeremiah that the city would be delivered into the hand of the king of Babylon's army, again came to Zedekiah and said: "We beseech thee, let this man be put to death: for thus he weakeneth the hands of the men of war that remain in this city, and the hands of all the people, in speaking such words unto them: for this man seeketh not the welfare of this people, but the hurt." Zedekiah again weakly yielded to these princes who were too strong for him; and this time Jeremiah was sentenced to a yet more terrible fate. The princes evidently feared to shed a prophet's blood; but thought that by letting him drown, or die of starvation, in the old abandoned well, they could accomplish their end and yet not be guilty of Jeremiah's blood. So they took him and lowered him with ropes far down into the dark and noisome well. There was no water in the well; but there was mud—"So Jeremiah sunk in the mire."

The old well and the mud in the bottom of it would have been the grave of Jeremiah had it not been for a humble slave, the Ethiopian eunuch, Ebedmelech. In some way he had come in contact with the great prophet and was impressed with his innocence and his righteous life. Perhaps, too, Jeremiah had done him some personal kindness. At all events, this Ethiopian slave went to the king and pleaded for the life of Jeremiah. The conscience of Zedekiah was undoubtedly troubled, and he seems to have been glad to yield to the supplication of Ebedmelech. He told him to take three men with ropes and rescue the prophet.

Ebedmelech was not only courageous in his plea for Jeremiah and compassionate in his consideration of him, but he was thoughtful and tender in the manner and method in which he delivered him. After his many imprisonments, Jeremiah was worn and emaciated, and Ebedmelech knew that the pull of the ropes under his armpits would cut and gall him. Therefore he lowered with the ropes old clouts, an old English word for rags, and with these improvised cushions between the ropes and his armpits, Jeremiah was gently drawn out of the pit. If he was familiar with Psalm 40—and undoubtedly he was— Jeremiah must have said to himself: "I waited patiently for the Lord; and He inclined unto me, and heard my cry. He brought me up also out of an horrible pit, out of the miry clay, and set my feet upon a rock, and established my goings. And He hath put a new song in my mouth, even praise unto our God. . . . Blessed is that man that maketh the Lord his trust." Delivered out of the prison, Jeremiah continued his fearless predictions and shared in the fate of Jerusalem when it fell.

This incident of Ebedmelech's merciful intervention is a bright ray of sunlight in the overcast and shadowed career of Jeremiah. Those who serve God are never altogether forgotten or forsaken; and sometimes their friends and deliverers appear in the most unlikely places. Who would have thought that the man to plead for Jeremiah and deliver him out of the prison would have been an attaché of the court of Zedekiah? and still less that his deliverer would have been an Ethiopian slave? Yet in the heart of this humble exile and slave God kindled the fire of compassion and friendship for his lonely and otherwise forsaken prophet.

It is pleasing to read that the gracious and courageous act of Ebedmelech was not forsaken. In the prophecies which God gave to Jeremiah, and which embraced the fall of a great city, the fall of a great kingdom, Babylon, and other nations such as Egypt, the future and the welfare of a single and very humble individual was not forgotten; for among his other prophecies Jeremiah was commissioned by God to go to Ebedmelech, the Ethiopian, saying, "Thus saith the Lord of hosts, the God of Israel; Behold, I will bring my words upon this city for evil, and not for good; and they shall be accomplished in that day before thee. But I will deliver thee in that day, saith the Lord: and thou shalt not be given into the hand of the man of whom thou art afraid. For I will surely deliver thee, and thou shalt not fall by the sword, but thy life shall be for a prey unto thee; because thou hast put thy trust in me, saith the Lord." Christ said, "He that receiveth a prophet in the name of a prophet, shall have a prophet's reward." He also said: "Whosoever shall give to drink unto one of these little ones a cup of cold water only, in the name of a disciple, verily, I say unto you, he shall in no wise lose his reward." Ebedmelech did not lose his reward.

ONESIPHORUS

Charles Dickens, in his story of *The Haunted Man*, tells of a gloomy, melancholy chemist who gladly accepted from a ghostly visitant the gift of oblivion. All that was bitter and painful in his thought of the past was gone, for memory was dead. But before long he found that the curse was greater than the blessing. The good vanished with the evil, and he became a specter and a plague, with power to purge other men of their memories, sweet and bitter. Two alone were able to resist his spell; one so bad and selfish that he had no pleasant memories to lose, and one so good and pure that he not only resisted the evil charm, but exorcised it from the breast of its unhappy owner. The story concludes with the words, "Lord, keep my memory green!"

There are times when memories of the past burn and oppress, for they may bring the sense of loss and pain and failure. To "raze out the written troubles of the brain," perhaps we might be tempted to close with such an offer as was made to the unfortunate man in the tale of the great master. But our lot would be as miserable as his. We should not know how important a part of life our memories of the past comprise until we had lost them. We should find that what we are is largely what we have been. We might lose a few memories of sorrow or failure, but all that is good and true and blessed in life, child joys, home pleasures, morning dreams and early aspirations would perish, too, and we should become as hollow ghosts. For,

> I am a part of all that I have met;
> Yet all experience is an arch wherethro'
> Gleams that untraveled world whose margin fades
> Forever and forever as I move.

Here we have a man who had just two possessions, memory and Luke, the beloved physician. "Only Luke is with me." In Paul's past there are many things that he might well have wished blotted out of his memory: the days when he blasphemed the Name and made others do likewise, when he was the chief of sinners. The days of his Christian experience, too, held many memories that must have been painful; the separation from his family, the enmity of the Jews, the persecution of Alexander, and other foes who tracked him over the world; and hardest of all, the desertion of those who had been his friends and disciples. But along with the bitter there was the recollection of things sweet and pleasant. Paul had been rich in his friendships and had grappled the souls of his friends to him with hooks of steel. In every suffering they had been his stay and comfort, and when he writes his letters he never fails to make mention of some of them. He never forgot a kindness, and when the troubles of life came in like a flood, and the night was darkest, he is still able to think of those who had helped him and done him kindness. So it is here in the last and loneliest hour of his life.

The letters written during the early period of Paul's captivity at Rome bear witness to his expectation of release and acquittal and a journey to Macedonia and Asia. This is confirmed by the evidence of the epistle to Titus, the letters to Timothy, and a very ancient and trustworthy tradition that Paul was set free and preached in Spain. He must have been absent from the city at the time of the great fire and savage Neronian persecutions. Somewhere in the east, at Troas, perhaps, or Niccopolis, in Epirus, Paul was rearrested, again appealed to Caesar and was once more taken to Rome. But this time it is a different captivity. Christianity has become an illegal faith, to be visited with death and obloquy. Instead of living in his own hired house and preaching freely, Paul is in the prison of a malefactor, without the ordinary comforts of life. He writes to Timothy at Ephesus in a very different tone from that of the other epistles. He now expects to take no journey save that into the "undiscovered country." For the first time we find in the great heart and mind no plan to go to Spain, or Asia, or Greece, or Jerusalem. He is now "ready to be offered up," and knows that the time of his departure is at hand. He asks only for a few comforts, his faded cloak, a few of his books, and the presence of Timothy. Tychicus he had sent to Ephesus; Titus had gone to Dalmatia; Crescens to Galatia; and Demas had forsaken him, having loved this present world. Only Luke is with him.

But Paul had once written, "in everything give thanks." And here in this hour of extremity he is able to give thanks. Among other things, he gives thanks for the friendship of Onesiphorus. At the beginning of his letter he wrote, "The Lord show mercy unto the household of Onesiphorus," and almost with his last words he said, "Salute the house of Onesiphorus."

Many another would have dwelt only on his own troubles and vexations and would have thought that he was therefore excused from making any mention of the other side of life. Sick people easily forget the many mercies which are theirs— the attention of those who love them, the ministry of the best skill and science, for a trifling sum, and wonderful discoveries which take the sting from pain. People who are in sorrow find it hard to persuade themselves that they have anything for which to be thankful. Men who have failed in an undertaking find it difficult to see any reason for gratitude. Yet all, if they searched the past and examined the present, would find some blessing in life and someone they ought to thank. Our blessings are dull and gray, until, on the wing, they show their beauty as they leave us. This was the fancy of Young:

> Like birds, whose beauties languish, half-conceal'd,
> Till, mounted on the wing, their glossy plumes
> Expanded, shine with azure, green and gold;
> How blessings brighten as they take their flight!

Onesiphorus was very likely an elder in the church at Ephesus. When Paul was on his way to Jerusalem, and the elders from Ephesus came down to bid him farewell at the port of Miletus, Onesiphorus may have been one of those who sorrowed most of all that they should see his face no more. He watched with sad heart that ship sail out into the bay, until it was lost in the distance. In the providence of God, the apprehensions of Paul were not realized, and it is almost certain that he did visit Ephesus again and saw his friends in that place, and among them Onesiphorus, who often refreshed him.

When Paul was arrested and taken again to Rome, Onesiphorus followed him there to seek him and find him. Paul says that he was not ashamed of his chains, but sought him diligently and found him. The change in the attitude of the Roman Empire toward Christianity made it dangerous for anyone openly to show himself a Christian or to show himself a friend of these "haters of mankind," as Tacitus called them. At his first hearing all his friends, with the exception of faithful Luke, had been frightened away from Paul. "At my first defense no one took my part." But this friend from far off Ephesus was not ashamed and not afraid. He was that kind of friend who is described in Proverbs, "A friend loveth at all times, and like a brother is born for adversity." Born for adversity! There is the highest praise that one friend can bestow upon another. With the passing of wealth, or with the passing of reputation, men have often found that a great many of their friends were not born for adversity. They are afraid of prisons and ashamed of chains.

In the great hall of one of the old time mansions of the Shenandoah valley there hangs the portrait of a broad-shouldered cavalier, and written in his own hand, are the words, "Yours to count on—J. E. B. Stuart." Among a great many of Paul's friends who were frightened and ashamed, and made shift to break their relationship with him, there was one upon whom he could count. The world's scorn, contempt, the probability of being thrown to a beast or covered with pitch and set on fire to illuminate the driveway of the emperor by night, never caused Onesiphorus to falter. It wasn't easy to find Paul; but he persisted in the search until he found him. There was no excuse which he could make to his conscience for not finding his old friend and ministering to him. Paul says, "He oft refreshed me"—literally, to "make cool"—as if he had poured cold water on his fevered head and feet.

On my first visit to Rome, after I had seen all the majestic and melancholy ruins of a world that was dead, I went to see the reputed prison of Paul, the Mamertine Dungeon. As I descended the Capitoline Hill I could see below me the Roman Forum, with the great arch of Septimus Severus confronting me, and the three mighty columns of the temple of the Castors rising in majesty over the sea of ruins. Under one of the churches on the hillside, I found the opening to the Mamertine Prison, and was admitted by the guard. If the Rome outside seemed to reek with antiquity, much more this subterranean prison. Here were imprisoned and strangled the noble Gaul, Vercingetorix; also the great African, Jugurtha. But a name greater than these brought me there. Like all dungeons of the old world, this one lies deep beneath the surface of the earth. As I descended the narrow winding stair, I wondered to myself—And did the weary feet of the great apostle take this same turning, and feel the damp as I now felt it in my bones? The dungeon consists of two chambers. The upper one is conical in shape, and through a round hole in the floor the prisoner was lowered to the dark and dismal place beneath. Here it was, perhaps, that Paul sent his last message to Timothy, telling him to come before winter, and to bring the cloak he had left at Troas. Here Luke the beloved physician ministered to his last necessities, and here it was that Onesiphorus, not ashamed of his chains, came to visit him and to refresh him.

The friendship of Onesiphorus was like a warm sunbeam finding its way into the lonely cell and lighting up the face of the doomed apostle. His ministry was like the song of a fountain which flows to heal and restore. Onesiphorus was willing to stake all for his friendship for Paul. Lord Brooks asked that they write on his tomb, "Here lies Sir Philip Sidney's friend." If Onesiphorus could have asked for an epitaph, I am sure it would have been this—"Here lies the friend of Paul!" And Paul might have said:

> Timotheus, when here and there you go
>   Through Ephesus upon your pastoral round,
>   Where every street to me is hallowed ground,
> I will be bold and ask you to bestow
> Kindness upon one home, where long ago
>   A helpmate lived, whose like is seldom found.
> And when the sweet spring flowers begin to blow,
>   Sometimes for me lay one upon his mound.
> Thus Paul long since from out his Roman cell,
>   As from the past he saw a face arise—
>   Fit picture of the veteran who surveys
> His yester years, waiting for the evening bell,
>   While Hesper shines within his quiet skies,
>   And memory fills with cheer his lonely days!

COMPARISON

Ebedmelech and Onesiphorus were both friends of great men and great servants of God. Themselves inconspicuous, their names are immortal because of their kindness to one of God's servants. Ebedmelech drew Jeremiah up out of the prison; Onesiphorus came to visit Paul in his dungeon and often refreshed him.

Both the Ethiopian eunuch and the disciple of Ephesus were men not ashamed of chains, and did not desert their friends when the world turned against them. When John Huss was being led out from the trial room at Constance, where he was burned to death, one of the lords standing in the crowd about the door, John of Chlum, stretched out his hand and took the hand of Huss. It was a courageous and beautiful act, and Huss afterward wrote how wonderful it was "to see Lord John not ashamed to hold out his hand to a poor abject heretic, a prisoner in chains and the butt of all men's tongues." Ebedmelech is a monument to the compassion. If one is in deep trouble or distress, one is fortunate if he has a loyal and faithful friend upon whom to depend. That has been proven over and over again, in prisons, dungeons, and on the field of battle.

Both men represent the fact that God's cause has loyal and faithful friends who will not be ashamed of it, and not afraid to testify to it, even under the most adverse circumstances. The Ethiopian went to Jeremiah in his cistern prison and Onesiphorus visited Paul in his dungeon. Never is the world left without someone who will hold out the cup of cold water in the name of the Lord Jesus Christ.

Ebedmelech and Onesiphorus are beautiful illustrations, too, of the fact that acts of courageous loyalty to God's cause and tenderness toward His servants will never be forgotten. Amid the prophecies which took in the fall of cities and the crash of empires, Jeremiah had one which dealt with the fate and safety of a single man, for in the fall of Jerusalem the Ethiopian eunuch was remembered and delivered from death. Onesiphorus, too, had his reward. We cannot be sure whether he is alive or dead when Paul sends him the lovely forget-me-not of his letter from the Roman prison. But, alive or dead, Onesiphorus had for his reward the prayers and supplications of a great apostle for his household and for himself, that in the Great Day—when all of us will need mercy—God would show mercy to Onesiphorus. What a reward is that, to have a man like Paul pray for you! Yet every Christian has the knowledge that One far greater than Paul is praying for him, for He for whom Paul was in prison ever lives to make intercession for us.

Christ, in His great prefiguration of the judgment, calls some to His side, saying to them, "I was in prison and ye came unto me, athirst and ye gave Me to drink." How sweet will be the music of that Voice to Ebedmelech the Ethiopian, and to Onesiphorus, who was not ashamed of the chains of Paul.

10

MANASSEH AND JOHN MARK

Manasseh is the prodigal son of the Old Testament. He had a great and godly father, and very likely a pious mother. He went into the far country and sinned and rebelled against God. There, like the prodigal, when he had suffered much he came to himself and said: "I have sinned against heaven and in thy sight." Having repented, he was forgiven and restored to his kingdom.

Manasseh was twelve years old when he began to reign, and he reigned fifty-five years in Jerusalem, the longest and the worst in the annals of the kingdom. In contrast with his great and noble father, Hezekiah, Manasseh did that which was evil in the sight of the Lord. The high places which his father had broken down he built again and reared altars for Baal worship and worshiped the host of heaven and served him. His own children he caused to pass through the fire in the valley of Hinnom. He consulted witches and dealt with familiar spirits and them that peep and mutter. All this infamy he crowned by setting up a carved image in the temple, the House of God, "of which," says the chronicler in his horror, God had said to David, "In this house, and in Jerusalem, which I have chosen out of all tribes of Israel, will I put my name forever."

Manasseh succeeded in making Israel worse than the heathen.

Warnings which came to him fell on deaf ears. At length, when his cup of iniquity was full, God punished him by bringing upon him the Assyrians, who bound him with fetters and carried him into Babylon. There Manasseh repented of his sins and besought the Lord and humbled himself greatly before the God of his fathers. God heard his prayers, accepted his repentance, and restored him to his kingdom. In the years that remained to him, Manasseh did all that he could to make amends for the great evil which he had done. Idols and strange gods were removed, the altar of the Lord repaired, and the sacrifices of peace offerings and thank offerings restored, and under his example and command Judah turned back to the worship of the true God. If one walking along the hanging gardens of Babylon had seen the helpless and mutilated Manasseh in his iron cage, with his face lacerated by the thorns and the hook, a sport for the Chaldean multitude, and had been told, "Manasseh will sit again upon the throne of David at Jerusalem," he would have answered that the thing was impossible. Yet this was the very thing which took place. All things are possible to repentance.

Manasseh is remembered by the chronicler, not only for his sins and his repentance, but for his prayer of repentance, which is twice mentioned, and which, he says, "is written among the sayings of the seers." The prayer of Manasseh is found in the Apocryphal Books of the Old Testament, between Bel and the Dragon and the first Book of the Maccabees. If any book in the Apocrypha is worthy of a place in the sacred literature of the church, the prayer of Manasseh is that book, for the prayer is a wonderful pouring out of a man's soul in accents of confession and repentance and supplication worthy of a David himself. The prayer is as follows:

> O Lord, Almighty God of our fathers, Abraham, Isaac, and Jacob, and of their righteous seed; who hast made heaven and earth, with all the ornament thereof; who hast bound the sea by the word of Thy commandment; who hast shut up the deep, and sealed it by Thy terrible and glorious name; whom all men fear, and tremble before Thy power; for the majesty of Thy glory cannot be borne, and Thine angry threatening toward

sinners is importable; but Thy merciful promise is unmeasurable and unsearchable!

Thou, O Lord, according to Thy great goodness hast promised repentance and forgiveness to them that have sinned against Thee: and of Thine infinite mercies hast appointed repentance unto sinners, that they may be saved. Thou therefore, O Lord, that art the God of the just, hast not appointed repentance to the just, as to Abraham, and Isaac, and Jacob, which have not sinned against Thee; but Thou hast appointed repentance unto me that am a sinner: for I have sinned above the number of the sands of the sea.

Now, therefore, I bow the knee of mine heart, beseeching Thee of grace. I have sinned, O Lord, I have sinned, and I acknowledge mine iniquities: wherefore I humbly beseech Thee, forgive me, O Lord, forgive me, and destroy me not with mine iniquities. Be not angry with me forever, by reserving evil for me; neither condemn me into the lower parts of the earth. For Thou art the God, even the God of them that repent; and in me Thou wilt shew all Thy goodness; for Thou wilt save me, that am unworthy, according to Thy great mercy. Therefore I will praise Thee forever all the days of my life: for all the powers of the heavens do praise Thee, and Thine is the glory forever and ever. Amen.

JOHN MARK

One of the great churches of the world is St. Mark's in Venice. According to a rather untrustworthy tradition, St. Mark's body was transported in the ninth century from Alexandria, where he died, to Venice, where a great church was built as a resting place for his dust. Venice rose in all its splendor and beauty out of the marshes and lagoons of the Adriatic Coast. The marsh became a great city. So St. Mark, at first weak, unreliable and unstable, finally emerges in the last part of his New Testament history a pillar of strength, a finished character, all his past failures overcome by perseverance, faith and the grace of God. He is one of those who "out of weakness were made strong." His symbol in church history is the lion. Strange that he who once was known as the quitter and the coward should now always appear before the world with the lion for his mark and sign.

The Gospel of St. Mark is the most vivid and graphic in style of all the Gospels. In the account of the arrest of Jesus at Gethsemane, Mark's Gospel alone has this most interesting fragment: "And there followed Him a certain young man having a linen cloth cast about his naked body; and the young man lay hold on Him, and he left the linen cloth and fled from them naked." This altogether incidental event, and yet very interesting one, has no occasion for being in the narrative, unless it is a personal reminiscence. It generally has been the supposition that the young man was none other than Mark himself. Aroused out of his sleep, perhaps, when the enemies of Christ came first to Mary's house to search for Jesus, Mark, throwing the linen cloth about his body and not waiting to dress, hurried to Gethsemane for the purpose of warning Jesus. He was too late for that, for Jesus was already in the hands of His enemies; but he followed along with the company on their way to the High Priest's house until some of the young men, suspecting him as a friend of Jesus, seized him, and Mark, leaving his garment in their clutches, fled from them naked.

When Christ prepared to eat the Passover with His disciples, He sent them into the city and told them that they would meet a man bearing a pitcher of water, whom they were to follow to his home. Some have thought that this man was Mark. But that is hardly likely, for the reference to the good man of the house would indicate that the man bearing the water pitcher was some kind of a servant.

Mark's mother was one of the famous Marys who appear in the history of Jesus and His disciples. From the account in Acts of Peter's escape from prison, we know that she was a woman of some means, for she had a house commodious enough to afford a meeting place for the Christian disciples at Jerusalem. As soon as Peter was out of the prison, he started for the house of Mary, for he was sure that the disciples would be praying for him there. In this he was not mistaken; and Luke gives us the interesting story of how he appeared at

Mary's door, and how the excited maid, named Rhoda, for gladness opened not the gate. Mark and Peter are associated in Christian tradition and in the history of the New Testament. Papias tells us that Mark was Peter's interpreter, and out of the knowledge gained from this companionship wrote his Gospel. Peter, in his first letter, sends the salutations of the church that is at Babylon, and then adds, "And so doth Marcus, my son." Whether or not by Babylon is meant the city on the Euphrates, or Rome, we cannot be sure; but the salutation shows a close personal and religious relationship between Peter and Mark. He calls him his son, just as Paul called Timothy his son. As Paul was responsible for the conversion of Timothy, so perhaps Peter was responsible for the conversion of Mark.

When Paul and Barnabas returned from Jerusalem to Antioch, after having carried an offering for the poor at Jerusalem, they took with them John Mark, who was either the cousin or nephew of Barnabas. Barnabas came of a well-to-do family of Cyprus, and that island probably was the ancestral seat of Mark's family.

When Paul and Barnabas set out from Selucia, the harbor of Antioch, on their epochal voyage, they took with them John Mark. He had not been designated by the Holy Spirit and set apart as Paul and Barnabas had been, but seems to have been taken along as a sort of an extra hand. The record is, "They had also John to their minister." There were many things which Mark in this capacity could do for the two older men, such as securing a lodging-place, and perhaps baptizing the converts. Mark was with Barnabas and Paul on the journey through the Island of Cyprus from Salamis to Paphos, and thence sailed with them to the city of Perga on the coast of Pamphylia.

Instead of remaining in the low country about Perga, which in the summer season is unhealthful, Paul went northward to the Galatian highlands. Some have thought that he had been taken sick at Perga with the epidemic malaria, and that it was this sickness which brought him to Galatia, and to which he refers in his letter to the Galatians when he says, "Ye know that because of an infirmity of the flesh, I preached the Gospel unto you the first time." Luke rarely gives any reason for the facts which he relates. All he says here is, "And John departing from them returned to Jerusalem."

Various motives have been assigned for the return of Mark, such as his jealousy of the leadership and influence of Paul, to whom Barnabas had now taken a second place; or that he was homesick for his mother and his friends; or that he had become discouraged, and did not believe that the heathen could be converted, or were worth converting; or that he was irresolute and unsettled in his mind; or that the original plan and arrangement had been to go no further than Pamphylia. But from what follows, the probability is that Mark had become alarmed at the dangers which would confront the missionaries as they proceeded from the coast into the robber-infested, mountainous country of the interior, for it was here Paul commenced his experience of those perils of robbers and perils of waters and perils of the wilderness to which he afterward refers in his catalog of woes. Perga was something of a port, and Mark would have no difficulty in finding a ship bound for Antioch. Thither he returned, and probably from Antioch went back to Jerusalem.

When Paul and Barnabas appeared in Jerusalem after their first missionary journey, at the first Council of the church, to plead for the Gentile Christians, Mark must have joined himself to them again. At all events, we read that after they had gone back to Antioch, and were planning to revisit the places touched on their first missionary journey, Barnabas proposed to take his nephew, Mark, with them again. To this Paul would not agree, because, Luke says, "Paul thought not good to take him with them, who departed from them from Pamphylia, and went not with them to the work." This unhappy contention and difference of opinion was so sharp that these two friends, who owed so much to one another, were separated. Barnabas took his nephew Mark and sailed for Cyprus, and Paul took Silas and went through Syria and Cilicia.

In a sense, both men were right. Paul was right in not wishing to have as a companion, in a difficult and dangerous journey, a man who had shown he lacked stamina and courage on the previous journey; and Barnabas was right in believing that his nephew had better possibilities in him and would give a better account of himself if he had the chance. Certainly, since they were unable to agree on the matter, Paul and Barnabas did the sensible thing when they separated. When two persons who are engaged in Christian work cannot agree as to plans and methods, instead of contending with each other and wasting the time in strife and recrimination, the wise and sensible thing for them to do is to separate and carry on their work in different places.

After we lose sight of Mark as he stands on the deck of that sailing vessel, bound for Salamis on the Isle of Cyprus, and, no doubt, feeling both sad and indignant over his rejection by Paul, we do not hear of him again for a decade, when we learn that he is with Peter at Babylon, for from Babylon, Peter, at the end of his first letter, sends to the Christians the greetings of that church, and of "Marcus, my son." There are good reasons for thinking that Babylon is Peter's name for Rome. If so, the probability is that Mark, after he had parted company with Barnabas, went back to Jerusalem and became the friend and attendant of Peter. Instead of becoming embittered or being cast into despair because of his rejection by Paul, Mark kept his Christian faith and soon showed himself worthy of trust and capable of important duties. It is hard enough for one to carry in his own conscience, like an old wound, the knowledge of some moral unworthiness or dishonorable deed, even when that unworthy thing is not known to others. It is still worse to be guilty of a dishonorable thing and to have everybody know it. This was Mark's misfortune. Paul had publicly declared him unworthy and unfit to be the companion of the heralds of the cross. He was a man who, having put his hand to the plow, looked backward and, therefore, Paul thought, was not fit for the great enterprise of carrying the gospel to the heathen. Laboring under this heavy handicap, Mark, nevertheless, acquitted himself with credit, became the worthy companion of Peter, and, as we shall see, passes from the stage of New Testament history as one of those whom Paul desires to have with him in his last hours at Rome.

In the letter to Philemon, among other salutations of his fellow-laborers, Paul sends the greetings of Marcus, evidently with him in that city; and in the conclusion of the letter to the

Colossians, also written at Rome, Paul sends the salutations of Marcus, and seems to refer to a previous letter or message to them concerning Mark, for he adds, "touching whom ye received commandments: if he come unto you, receive him." The supposition is that Mark's reputation as a quitter and deserter had spread through the church, and that these Christians at Colossae were reluctant to receive him as a brother to be trusted. Therefore Paul is careful to say a word on his behalf.

Mark passes from history, magna cum laude, in Paul's last message to the world, the second letter to Timothy. In this letter he tells Timothy to come to him, and to come before winter. Then he adds, "Take Mark and bring him with thee, for he is profitable to me for the ministry." Mark's conduct had been such as completely to reinstate him in the confidence and in the affection of Paul. That fine farewell is a credit, not only to Mark, but also to Paul, who showed himself large enough and magnanimous enough to overcome a prejudice toward one who once had proved himself unworthy at a critical moment, but who, by his subsequent conduct had demonstrated that he had other qualities than those of a quitter and a deserter.

COMPARISON

Manasseh and Mark were both men who, in the terms of the street, "came back." Both were singularly fortunate in their early environment and religious opportunities. Manasseh was a son of one of the greatest and best kings of Judah, Hezekiah; and Mark was the nephew of one of the noblest men of the New Testament, Barnabas, and the son of a noble and distinguished woman, Mary. Yet both men at first prostituted their gifts and wasted their opportunities. Manasseh sold himself to every wickedness in his long and notorious reign; and Mark, while not a transgressor in that sense, yet failed dismally as the companion of heroic Paul on the first missionary journey. Frightened and dismayed at the perils of the Galatian hinterland, Mark quit Paul and Barnabas and went home. The world will forgive a man almost every offense and weakness but that of cowardice.

Both men were great in their repentance. In his captivity, Manasseh besought the Lord his God and "humbled himself greatly before the God of his fathers, and prayed unto Him and He was entreated of him, and heard his supplication and brought him again to Jerusalem into his kingdom." There Manasseh, restored to his kingdom, spent his last days trying to undo the great wickedness that he had done. He repaired the altars he had overthrown, and destroyed the idols which he had set up in the Holy City and in the holy place. Repentance, too, plays its part and sings its great song in the life of Mark, for we cannot think of Mark, once branded by Paul as a quitter and a coward, but now invited to come to him to strengthen him and companion him in the prison of Rome, without being convinced that he had sincerely repented of his sin of weakness and cowardice. He had brought forth the fruits of a true repentance, and both Peter and Paul were glad to recognize those fruits and to honor Mark as a friend and companion, profitable and helpful, and a true follower of Jesus Christ.

Both Manasseh and Mark show what can be done with lives which have been hurt and marred by sin. The alchemists had a theory of some acid which, poured over rubbish, could transmute the rubbish to the purest gold. What is only a fancy in chemistry is beautifully true in the chemistry of the soul. The acid of repentance poured over a broken, stained and marred life, is able to restore that life to the image of God.

During the World War, British Army bulletins told of a certain Colonel Elkington, who, in the early period of the War was cashiered from the army for conduct unbecoming an officer. The public dispatches did not state the nature of his misconduct; but the inference was that it was cowardice in the face of the enemy. The disgraced officer, whose name had been dropped from the rolls of the British Army, went to Paris, where he assumed another name and enlisted in the Foreign Legion. Whenever the men of this Legion went into action, this man was conspicuous for his daring and gallantry. After one of these heroic exploits he was decorated by the government of France. In some way his real identity was disclosed and the facts brought to the attention of the British Government. His commission was given back to him and, resuming his name and rank, he again joined his regiment at the front. By wounds, courage and fidelity, he won back the honors and the rank which his cowardice had lost him. So Manasseh and Mark, by their repentance and their devotion to duty, won back their place in the esteem of their contemporaries, and their names will be known and honored as long as men read the Bible and believe in God.

In the chapel of a certain church there is a bronze tablet on the wall to the memory of a former superintendent of the Sunday School. The inscription on the tablet tells of the deep affection and high regard in which this man was held by the officers and members of that Sunday School. One day, the minister pondered over a letter asking for a character reference for this man. He knew that where the man had formerly been employed he had proven himself unworthy of confidence, and had stolen from his employers. The problem was how to give this man a second chance. In some way that problem was solved and the man got with a new employer a second chance. Of the way in which he used that second chance, and how splendidly he "came back," that tablet on the church's wall is the fine and enduring record.

Both Manasseh and Mark were men who did not sin to themselves. The later writers and prophets attributed Judah's misfortune and captivity to the sin and apostasy of Manasseh. Mark's moral failure brought on a sad dispute and feud between two great men of God, Barnabas and Paul. This presents to us a very arresting thought about a man's transgression. If a man could take upon himself all the results and punishments of his sin, it would not be so appalling; but no man can do that. When 'tis done, 'tis not done. Adam sinned, and the ground was cursed for his sake. Manasseh sinned, and all Israel suffered with him. Mark sinned, and separated those fast friends, Barnabas and Paul.

Two brothers were once convicted of stealing sheep. It was in a day of cruel judicial punishments, and the magistrate sentenced them to be branded on the forehead with the letters ST, which stood for Sheep Thief.

One of the brothers, unable to bear the stigma, tried to bury himself in a foreign land. But the people would read the letters on his brow and ask him what they meant. Thus he was driven from land to land, and at length, full of bitterness, he died and was buried in a forgotten grave.

The other brother also repented of his crime. But instead of going away, he said, "I can't run away from the fact that I stole sheep, and here I will remain until I win back the respect of my neighbors and myself." Years passed, and as they passed he succeeded in establishing a reputation for probity and honor. One day a stranger, coming to the town, saw the old man with the letters ST branded on his forehead, and asked a native what they signified. The native thought for a little, and then said, "It all happened a great while ago, and I have forgotten the particulars; but I think the letters are an abbreviation of Saint."

11

Hannah And Mary

The mothers of the Bible constitute a glorious company. This long roll commences with Eve, the mother of all living, includes Sarah, Rebecca, Rizpah, who watched day and night, keeping the birds and the beasts away from the bodies of her sons who had been hanged by David; the Shunammite woman, whose son Elisha restored to life; Jochebed, the mother of Moses; Elisabeth, the mother of John the Baptist; and comes to a climax with Mary, the mother of our Lord. Not the least in this goodly order of devout and pious mothers is Hannah, the mother of Samuel.

Many of these mothers had to pass through the trial of long waiting for a child. Abraham and Sarah, Isaac and Rebecca, the Shunammite woman, Zacharias and Elisabeth, and Elkanah and Hannah were all, for a time, without a child. So often does this occur in the history of redemption, that whenever we read that a certain man and woman had no child, we are prepared to expect the opening of a great chapter in God's goodness and grace.

It was so in the history of Israel, in the degenerate days of Eli. Elkanah, living on Mt. Ephraim, had two wives, Penninah and Hannah. Elkanah was evidently prosperous, well-to-do, and his house abounded with comforts. Yet his home was not a happy one, for the wife whom he loved was childless. The chronicler tells us that Elkanah gave to Penninah and to all her sons and daughters portions, but to Hannah he gave a worthy portion, for he loved Hannah. Disappointment was bad enough for Hannah; but under peculiar circumstances it was doubly trying, for her rival Penninah, the mother of children, taunted the unhappy woman with her barrenness. It must have been a sad home in which to live. It must have been hard, too, for Elkanah, with the wife he loved sad-eyed and weeping, and the other wife taunting her and mocking her. Elkanah did what he could to make the situation better, and said to Hannah, "Hannah, why weepest thou? and why eatest thou not? and why is thy heart grieved? Am I not better to thee than ten sons?" That was a gentle, kind, and compassionate speech for Elkanah to make to brokenhearted Hannah. But I suppose, had he been a woman, he would never have asked the last question, "Am I not better to thee than ten sons?" for he had left out of the reckoning the tender, elemental and mighty fact, the urge of maternity.

Yet, through all this trying period, Elkanah did not neglect his religious duties. With his two wives he went regularly up to the holy house at Shiloh to offer sacrifice to the Lord of hosts. Some people, when they get into personal or domestic difficulties, quit the church and give up their religion; but not so Elkanah. Every year he took his divided household up to Shiloh. On this occasion, after the sacrifice had been made in the tabernacle, and Elkanah and Penninah and the rest of the family had gone out, Hannah remained behind. "In the bitterness of her soul she prayed unto the Lord and wept sore." A short verse that is; yet a marvelous portrait of a human soul in distress. In her prayer Hannah said, "O Lord of hosts, if Thou wilt indeed look on the affliction of Thine handmaid and remember me and not forget Thine handmaid, but wilt give unto Thine handmaid a man child, then I will give him unto the Lord all the days of his life."

This brief, but intensely earnest, prayer, Hannah repeated many times, until her voice failed her, and she went on praying in her heart, her lips moving, but no sound coming therefrom. Awakening out of his sleep upon his seat near a post in the tabernacle, the old priest, Eli, unaccustomed to seeing people praying earnestly in that degenerate day, and thinking Hannah was some woman who had taken too much wine at the sacrifice, said gruffly to her, "How long wilt thou be drunken? Put away thy wine from thee." But Eli had made a sad mistake. Earnestness had been taken for drunkenness, and the fine frenzy of the soul for the intoxication of wine. The people of Jerusalem thought that Peter and the apostles, so enthusiastic about Christ and the gospel, must be men who were filled with new wine. Eli thought that any woman moving her lips, but uttering no sound, must be drunken and dissolute. It shows how even a good man in a good place could be wholly and cruelly wrong in his judgment upon another person. In one form or another, the mistake of Eli is constantly being repeated, and sensitive souls are hurt, and lives made unhappy through these hasty verdicts and snap judgments of our fallible human understanding. Eli's race is not extinct. Many of the judgments which we pass, with more or less severity, are based upon imperfect knowledge, yet we rush into judgment as if we were omniscient.

Among the legends that have come down about Professor Blaikie, of Edinburgh, is the story that when a student arose one day to recite in the classroom, he held his book in his right hand. Blaikie told him to take the book in his left hand. But the student continued to read with the book held in his right hand. In a passion, Blaikie thundered at him to take the book with his left hand. "I cannot, sir," answered the student, as he brought from behind his back an empty sleeve. The students hissed, but the next moment cheered, when the famous Grecian made earnest apology. Lips that move and do not speak, sleeves that have no arm within, purple garments outside, like the king on Samaria's wall, and sackcloth within— this is life. Yet we continue to register our rash judgments founded upon impressions that are not reliable. If we saw all that God sees we might have to reverse many of our verdicts. We should be surprised to learn how one man carried a load that we never imagined; how another had things to aggravate him and irritate him which we never saw; and how another was fighting a grim battle with sorrow or with sin, while we, from the place of our ease and comfort and ignorance, were passing bitter judgment upon his conduct.

> If we knew the cares and trials,
>   Knew the efforts all in vain;
> And the bitter disappointment,
>   Understood the loss and gain—
> Would the grim eternal roughness
>   Seem, I wonder, just the same?
> Should we help where now we hinder?
>   Should we pity where we blame?
>
> Could we but draw back the curtains
>   That surround each other's lives.
> See the naked heart and spirit,
>   Know what spur the spirit gives.
> Often we should find it better,
>   Purer than we judged we should.
> We should love each other better
>   If we only understood.

Realizing the sad mistake he had made—for Hannah had answered him, "I am a woman of a sorrowful spirit. I have drunk neither wine nor strong drink, but have poured out my soul before the Lord"—Eli made haste to change his tone, and said to her, "Go in peace: and the God of Israel grant thee thy petition that thou hast asked of him." In the course of time, Hannah's prayer was answered and a son was born to her and Elkanah. Faithful to her vow, Hannah, when her child was weaned, took him up to Shiloh and left him in charge of the priests. Every year she would go up with a little garment for the growing lad.

The heart that once was sad and broken now rejoiced. Her tears were turned into laughter, and Hannah prayed again to the Lord, but this time it was a song of rejoicing:

> And Hannah prayed, and said, My heart rejoiceth in the Lord, mine horn is exalted in the Lord: my mouth is enlarged over mine enemies; because I rejoice in Thy salvation. There is none holy as the Lord; for there is none beside Thee: neither is there any rock like our God. Talk no more so exceeding proudly; let not arrogancy come out of your mouth: for the

Lord is a God of knowledge, and by him actions are weighed. The bows of the mighty men are broken, and they that stumbled are girded with strength. They that were full have hired out themselves for bread; and they that were hungry ceased; so that the barren hath born seven; and she that hath many children is waxed feeble. The Lord maketh poor, and maketh rich: He bringeth low, and lifteth up. He raiseth up the poor out of the dust, and lifteth up the beggar from the dunghill, to set them among princes, and to make them inherit the throne of glory; for the pillars of the earth are the Lord's, and He hath set the world upon them. He will keep the feet of His saints, and the wicked shall be silent in darkness; for by strength shall no man prevail. The adversaries of the Lord shall be broken to pieces; out of heaven shall He thunder upon them: the Lord shall judge the ends of the earth; and He shall give strength unto His King, and exalt the horn of His anointed.

After this, we read that Eli blessed Elkanah and his wife and promised them more children in return for the loan which they had made to the Lord in giving Him Samuel. Hannah became the mother of three other sons and two daughters. Who they were, and what they were, we know not; but Hannah had made herself immortal by giving to Israel a man who, in a day of wickedness and unbelief, was to revive the nation's faith and bring it back to God.

MARY

On the cross, probably the last face which our Lord saw was the face of His mother, Mary, standing, as devout old Simeon had once predicted, with a sword through her heart as she watched her expiring Son. John writes how when Jesus saw His mother, He said, referring to John, "Woman, behold thy son!" and to John, "Behold thy mother." Having finished His earthly ministry with this beautiful act of filial devotion and affection, Jesus gave up the ghost. This last record ought to clear up any difficulties as to a possible abruptness of manner or lack of feeling on the part of Jesus in His dealings with His mother. We can be sure that He who came into the world through the mysterious gateway of motherhood was not unmindful of the ties which bound Him to this woman and, forever afterward, to all women.

Here and there, prophecy had hinted at the birth of Jesus, but the great mass of people either were not expecting Him at all, or were expecting Him to make His advent in some other and more spectacular way.

> They all were looking for a king,
>   To slay their foes and lift them high,
> Thou camest a little baby thing,
>   That made a woman cry.

When Mary, filled with wonder, came to visit the other mother expectant, her kinswoman Elisabeth, Elisabeth cried out:

> Blessed art thou among women, and blessed is the fruit of thy womb. And whence is this to me, that the mother of my Lord should come to me? For lo, as soon as the voice of Thy salutation sounded in mine ears, the babe leaped in my womb for joy. And blessed is she that believed; for there shall be a performance of those things which were told her from the Lord.

It was foretold that a great prophet would prepare the way for Christ. This prophet, Jesus said, was John the Baptist. Thus, even before either was born, John saluted and hailed the coming King and Redeemer. Then Mary answered the Benedictus of Elisabeth with her own glorious Magnificat, and said:

> My soul doth magnify the Lord, and my spirit hath rejoiced in God my Savior. For He hath regarded the low estate of His handmaiden: for, behold, from henceforth all generations shall call me blessed. For He that is mighty hath done to me great things; and holy is His name. And His mercy is on them that fear Him from generation to generation. He hath shewed strength with His arm; He hath scattered the proud in the imagination of their hearts. He hath put down the mighty from their seats, and exalted them of low degree. He hath filled the

hungry with good things; and the rich He hath sent empty away. He hath holpen His servant Israel in remembrance of His mercy; as He spake to our fathers, to Abraham, and to his seed forever.

The next scene shows us Mary with the Child in her arms when she brought Him up to the temple to present Him to the Lord. Filled with the Spirit, the devout old priest Simeon took the Child in his arms and blessed Him, saying:

> Lord, now lettest thou Thy servant depart in peace, according to Thy word: for mine eyes have seen Thy salvation, which Thou hast prepared before the face of all people; a light to lighten the Gentiles, and the glory of Thy people Israel. . . . Behold, this Child is set for the fall and rising again of many in Israel; and for a sign which shall be spoken against; (Yea, a sword shall pierce through thy own soul also,) that the thoughts of many hearts may be revealed.

In the quiet chamber in the gallery at Dresden, which one enters as if it were a chapel of devotion, one looks on the face of Mary and the face of the Child Jesus as Raphael has forever photographed them in the Sistine Madonna. The Child, who is held in the mother's arms, has about Him more than the look of a child; rather the look of a king and ruler; while the mother's eyes seem to be fixed earnestly, almost fearfully, at some object in the distance, as if wondering at the mysterious predictions of Simeon, how this Child was set for the fall and rising of many in Israel.

The next time we see Mary is twelve years later, when they go up to Jerusalem to worship and sacrifice. When they started home, Jesus remained in the temple. His mother and Joseph, supposing that He was somewhere in the company of people who had gone up from Nazareth, went on a day's journey, but when they found Him not they went back to the city to search for Him. After a three days' hunt they found Him in the temple sitting in the midst of the doctors, both hearing them and asking them questions. When they saw Him, His mother said to Him:

Son, why hast Thou thus dealt with us? behold, Thy father and I have sought Thee sorrowing. And He said unto them, How is it that ye sought Me? wist ye not that I must be about my Father's business?

But they understood not the saying which He spoke to them. How many things about this mysterious Child the Virgin Mother was not able to understand, both before and after His birth!

Comparison

When the angel announced the birth of Jesus to the Virgin, and the perplexed Mary wondered how these things could be, Gabriel said to her, "With God nothing shall be impossible." Both the birth of Samuel and the birth of Jesus let us know that with God nothing shall be impossible. The great miracle is God Himself.

> Admit a God—that mystery supreme!
> That cause uncaused! All other wonders cease:
> Nothing is marvelous for Him to do;
> Deny Him—all is mystery besides.

Both Hannah and Mary were highly honored of the Lord. Hannah was chosen to be the mother of the child who, as a man, was to revive true religion among the people of Israel; and Mary was chosen to be the mother of our Lord. Both women were chosen of God, but not without reason. So far as a mere birth was concerned, God could have accomplished that through any other woman of the time of Samuel, or when Jesus was born. But the women chosen to be the mothers of these great actors in the drama of redemption were both women who feared the Lord, and women of devotion and of great faith. When we begin to plan for the future of the world, we must begin with the mother, and before the child is born. Certainly it was not an accident that Byron's mother was a passionate virago; or that Nero's mother was a murderess; or that Augustine's mother was a woman of many prayers; or that the mother of the Wesleys was often upon her knees.

Both Hannah and Mary passed through periods of bitterness of soul; Hannah, before her child was born, when Penninah taunted her with her barrenness; and Mary, after her Child was born, when He had become a man and was taking His lonely way to Gethsemane and Golgotha.

Both were women of great faith. It took great faith for the fruitless Hannah to believe that the prayers she had offered in the house at Shiloh would be answered. Perhaps it took greater faith for the Virgin to believe that what the angel told her would come to pass, and when it had come to pass, that the strange thing which had happened to her was of the Lord.

Both were faithful mothers. The best father and the best mother in the world cannot insure a noble manhood or womanhood for their child. But when they have presented the child to the Lord, have prayed for it and with it, and brought it up in the nurture and admonition of the Lord, and daily set before it an example of godly living, that is all that any father or mother can do. The rest must be left to the child—and to God. These two mothers were faithful to the high responsibility which God had laid upon them, for we see them both at the holy place, one in the tabernacle, the other in the temple, giving their child back to the Lord.

When we tell the story of these two great mothers, we must not forget the kind of husbands they had. Where will you find a more thoughtful or kinder husband than Hannah had in Elkanah? This good man, no doubt perplexed and distraught at the disharmony in his home, did all that he could to strengthen and comfort the sad and disappointed Hannah, saying to her, "Why is thy heart grieved? Am I not better to thee than ten sons?" Joseph is worthy of having his name written as high up on the roll of noble husbands as that of Elkanah. No husband was ever put in a more difficult position. If it took faith for Mary to believe what the angel had told her about the Child which was to be born to her, I think it took almost greater faith for Joseph to believe what the angel of the Lord said to him in a dream, that he was not to hesitate to take the espoused virgin Mary for his wife, and that that which was conceived in her was of the Holy Spirit.

Joseph was a man of great faith. But he was a man of great

kindness and justice also. Even if we did not have that record, how when the day came he obeyed the angel and took Mary to him as his wife, we should know that he was a noble and magnanimous man, well fitted for the high honor of being the husband of her who was to be the mother, not of his own child, but of the Son of God; for we are told that when he learned the condition of Mary, being a just man and not willing to make her a public example, he was "minded to put her away privily." Amid all the characters in that wonderful group who gather around the new-born Babe of Bethlehem, black-faced sinister Herod, the adoring shepherds, the Magi, the old priests Zacharias and Simeon, and the godly women Elisabeth and Anna, we must not forget the noble, kind and magnanimous Joseph, a "just man."

12

ZEDEKIAH AND PILATE

The last chapter in the history of the Hebrew monarchy makes melancholy reading. After Nebuchadnezzar had set up and then set aside two kings, he stripped the land of its soldiers, its workmen, and its artisans, and set up as king, Mattanniah, a son of the great and good Josiah, whose name he changed to Zedekiah, which means "the justice of the Lord."

Zedekiah was twenty-one years old when he began to reign and he reigned eleven years in Jerusalem, not as an independent king, but as the creature of Nebuchadnezzar. Into these eleven years he packed a great deal of iniquity. The chronicler records of him:

> And he did that which was evil in the sight of the Lord his God, and humbled not himself before Jeremiah the prophet speaking from the mouth of the Lord. And he also rebelled against King Nebuchadnezzar, who had made him swear by God: but he stiffened his neck, and hardened his heart from turning unto the Lord God of Israel. Moreover all the chief of the priests, and the people, transgressed very much after all the abominations of the heathen: and polluted the house of the Lord which he had hallowed in Jerusalem. And the Lord God of their fathers sent to them by his messengers, rising up betimes, and sending; because He had compassion on His

people, and on His dwelling place: but they mocked the messengers of God, and despised His words, and misused His prophets, until the wrath of the Lord arose against His people, till there was no remedy.

Disregarding the counsel of the prophet Jeremiah, Zedekiah revolted against Nebuchadnezzar in the ninth year of his reign. For two years Nebuchadnezzar besieged Jerusalem, during which period there was great famine and suffering in the city. In an effort to escape, Zedekiah led a night sortie from Jerusalem, but was overtaken by the Chaldeans and routed near Jericho, and brought before Nebuchadnezzar at Riblah. Nebuchadnezzar slew Zedekiah's two sons in his presence, put out his eyes, bound him in irons and carried him captive to Babylon. Such was the sunset of the once glorious kingdom of David, and such was the dismal fate of the last of the kings of Judah.

During the siege of Jerusalem by the Babylonians, Zedekiah saw a great deal of the prophet Jeremiah. The patriotic party, aided by false prophets, were advocating continued resistance to the king of Babylon. One of these false prophets, Hannaniah, predicted the complete deliverance of the city and the nation out of the hand of Nebuchadnezzar. In this prophecy he said, "Thus speaketh the Lord of hosts, the God of Israel, saying, I have broken the yoke of the king of Babylon. Within two full years will I bring again into this place all the vessels of the Lord's house, that Nebuchadnezzar king of Babylon took away from this place, and carried them to Babylon; And I will bring again to this place Jeconiah the son of Jehoiakim king of Judah, with all the captives of Judah, that went into Babylon, saith the Lord; for I will break the yoke of the king of Babylon." When he had finished this prediction, Hannaniah, in order to give the people a sign, took a yoke from off the neck of Jeremiah and broke it, for so, he said, God would break within two full years the yoke of Babylon from off the neck of all the nations then oppressed by that kingdom. For answer, Jeremiah said: "Thus saith the Lord: Thou hast broken the bars of wood, but thou hast made in their stead bars of iron." The prophet then denounced Hannaniah and predicted his death as a judgment for his rebellion against the word of God.

If Zedekiah was disposed to give heed to the word of the false prophet, he nevertheless seemed to realize all the time that the true prophet who was speaking the Word of God was Jeremiah. The counsel of Jeremiah to submit to Babylon made him the object of bitter hatred on the part of the firebrands and zealous nationalists. When Jeremiah was leaving the city for a visit, his enemies had him arrested and charged with desertion and treason. This charge Jeremiah stoutly denied, saying, "It is false. I am not falling away to the Chaldeans." But despite his protest, the leaders of the patriotic party beat Jeremiah and cast him into the prison in the house of Jonathan.

After Jeremiah had languished many days in the dungeon, Zedekiah had him brought to the palace secretly and had an interview with him. He said to him: "Is there any word from the Lord?" The question shows that the king knew in his heart that Jeremiah was the true prophet of God. Publicly, he would not recognize him as a prophet; but privately he did so. Jeremiah had a chance to escape the prison by prophesying some smooth thing, such as deliverance from the king of Babylon. But, faithful to his commission, he said bluntly to the king: "There is. Thou shalt be delivered into the hand of the king of Babylon." Then Jeremiah besought Zedekiah not to recommit him to the dungeon. In answer to this appeal, the king had him committed to the court of the guard of the prison, evidently a less severe imprisonment.

The princes of the people, not satisfied to leave Jeremiah alive, now demanded of the king that he be put to death on the ground that his prophecies had weakened the hands of the defenders of the city and that he was seeking not the welfare of the people, but their hurt. The weak and hesitating Zedekiah, although he knew the prophet to be innocent, yielded to the demands of these princes, saying as he did so, "Behold he is in your hand; for the king is not he that can do anything against you." This time they took Jeremiah and lowered him to the bottom of an abandoned well, where he sank in the mire, and soon would have perished, had it not been for the kind and fearless intervention of the Ethiopian eunuch, Ebedmelech.[1]

---

1. See Ebedmelech and Onesiphorus, chapter 9.

When the eunuch made his plea to Zedekiah, the king, evidently troubled in conscience, was glad to yield to his supplication, and sent thirty men to draw Jeremiah out of the well where his enemies had left him to perish. When he had been brought out of the dungeon, the perplexed monarch again sought the counsel of Jeremiah, saying to him: "I will ask thee a thing; hide nothing from me." Jeremiah responded, "If I declare it unto thee, wilt thou not surely put me to death? and if I give thee counsel, wilt thou not hearken unto me?" But Zedekiah swore secretly unto the prophet that he would not put him to death, neither deliver him into the hand of his enemies. Thus assured, Jeremiah told the king that if he would go forth and surrender to the king of Babylon, he would save not only his own soul, but the city from destruction. If he remained in the city and resisted Nebuchadnezzar, then the city would be destroyed and Zedekiah himself would be delivered into the hands of the Chaldeans. As an excuse for not doing as the prophet advised, Zedekiah said he feared that he would suffer injury and insult at the hands of the Jews who were now with the Chaldean army. But Jeremiah assured him that this would not be. "Obey, I beseech thee, the voice of the Lord, which I speak unto thee: so it shall be well unto thee, and thy soul shall live."

Evidently in great fear for his life, Zedekiah bound Jeremiah to secrecy concerning their interview and thus they parted. It would have been well for the unhappy king had he followed his conscience instead of his fears. Afraid to stay in the city, and unwilling to obey Jeremiah, Zedekiah made his foolish attempt to escape through the lines of the Chaldean army, and being captured and brought before Nebuchadnezzar, had his eyes put out and was carried down to Babylon. Such was the miserable climax to the king's vacillation, hesitation, and foolish efforts to evade the commandment of the Lord. It is difficult to write history with an "if"; but had Zedekiah followed the counsel of Jeremiah, the city would have been spared and his life saved.

PILATE

Every visitor to Rome pays a visit to the Scala Sancta, the supposed marble stairway of the judgment seat, at the foot of which Jesus stood on trial before Pontius Pilate. The name of Pilate is more frequently spoken throughout Christendom than that of any character in the New Testament, for in the Apostles' Creed we confess that our Lord "suffered under Pontius Pilate." The time element in the atonement is indicated by that phrase of the Apostles' Creed. Standing before the marble stairway of Rome—and whether it be the real stairway or not makes little difference—one cannot help thinking of the battle of conscience which was waged there in the breast of the Roman governor, before Pilate finally surrendered and delivered Jesus up to be crucified.

Awakened early on that fateful morning by the tumult at the gates of his palace, Pilate went forth to meet the Jews, little thinking that this was his day of destiny. When he heard the accusation that the solitary prisoner before him was perverting the nation, forbidding tribute to Caesar, and claiming that he was a king, Pilate at once had the conviction, or intuition, that the scribes and Pharisees were hypocrites and that Christ was innocent. He at once began his effort to evade jurisdiction in the case. First, he told the Jews to take Jesus and judge Him according to their own law. But here he was baffled by their answer that under the Roman law they did not have the power of capital punishment. Pilate then took Jesus into his chambers and had a private interview with Him. Pilate was everything that was bad; the sort of man who had not hesitated to mingle the blood of the Galileans with the blood of sacrifice. Yet in the presence of Jesus, Pilate's better nature rose to the surface. When he asked Jesus, "Art thou the King of the Jews?" Jesus responded, "Sayest thou this of thyself, or did others tell it thee of me?" Pilate haughtily disavowed any interest in the kingship of Jesus, saying abruptly and scornfully, "Am I a Jew? Thine own nation and the chief priests have delivered Thee unto me: what hast Thou done?" Jesus answered, "My kingdom is not of this world." Pilate then quickly forgot his feigned lack of interest and said, "Art thou a king, then?" to which

Jesus responded, "To this end was I born, and for this cause came I into the world, that I should bear witness unto the truth. Every one that is of the truth heareth my voice." At that, Pilate exclaimed, "What is truth?" In the opening sentence of his celebrated essay on *Truth*, Francis Bacon took the view that Pilate was only jesting. "'What is truth?' said jesting Pilate, and would not stay for an answer." I am not sure that this was so. Perhaps it was a half-sad, half-bitter confession on the part of Pilate that truth had escaped him, a sort of aside, to himself, rather than to Christ—"What *is* truth?"

Having asked the unanswered question, Pilate brought the interview to an end and went out before the people and said, "I find no crime in Him." He is interested only in the truth. He is no pretender to your Jewish throne or to Caesar's. At this, the Jews, fearful of losing their prey, called out, "He stirreth up the people, teaching throughout all Judea and beginning from Galilee unto this place." When he heard the word, Galilee, Pilate caught at it as a chance to shift jurisdiction in this case to Herod, under whose immediate jurisdiction Galilee was. Herod happened to be in Jerusalem, and off to him Pilate dispatched Jesus. In that memorable interview, Herod, who was anxious to ask Jesus many questions, saw his curiosity go unsatisfied, for Jesus "answered him not a word." Thus baffled and foiled, Herod arrayed Him in a scarlet robe as a sign of mockery and sent Him back to Pilate.

Just as Pilate was ascending his judgment seat to deal once more with this troublesome case, a slave brought him a message from his wife. The message read, "Have nothing to do with that just man, for I have suffered many things this night in a dream because of Him." To save Pilate from the sin of delivering Jesus over to His enemies, even the supernatural world whispered in his ear. Disturbed at the dream of his wife, Pilate once more announced the innocence of Jesus, saying that neither he nor Herod could find anything in Him worthy of death. Then Pilate, suddenly remembering the custom of releasing some notorious prisoner at the time of the feast, suggested that the people permit him to release the King of the Jews. With that they set up a shout, "Not this man; but Barabbas!" Barabbas was in prison for murder and insurrection.

Baffled again, and the more entangled the more he hesitated, Pilate thought he might escape the guilt of delivering Jesus over to be crucified by having Him scourged. So he said to the people, "I have found no cause of death in Him. I will therefore chastise Him and let Him go." When Jesus had been scourged, Pilate brought Him out again before the people. On His brow was the crown of thorns; the seamless robe covered His lacerated back and shoulders; while the blood from His wounds stained the white marble of the judgment steps. Pilate thought this spectacle would certainly appease the Jews. But the sight of His blood only stirred them to the greater rage and madness. In answer to Pilate's, "Behold the man!" as if to say, "Here is no pretender or king. Are not His sufferings now sufficient to satisfy your animosity?" the mob cried out, "Crucify Him! Crucify Him!"

Still unwilling to surrender, Pilate had a second private interview with Jesus. He had heard the Jews say, "We have a law, and by that law He ought to die because He made Himself the Son of God." The Son of God! That startled Pilate and seemed to confirm all his convictions that he was having to do with no ordinary prisoner. What if, indeed, He were a divine being, a Son of God? "Whence art Thou?" said the troubled Governor to the prisoner before him. But Jesus answered him not. Then Pilate, in indignation, said, "Knowest Thou not that I have power to crucify Thee?" At that, Jesus broke the silence and said, "Thou couldst have no power at all against me, except it were given thee from above." This answer shook Pilate to the depths of his being. His first impression, the strange answers of the prisoner, the message of his wife's dream, all had served to warn Pilate not to do anything against this Man. Again he made one more effort to release Jesus, and bringing Him forth, said, "Behold your King!" But the only answer from the Jews was, "Away with Him, away with Him, crucify Him!" Still Pilate drew back from giving the fatal word. Then one voice, more strident and raucous than the others, exclaimed: "If thou release this Man, thou art not Caesar's friend!" Caesar's friend! Son of God!—Which now will have the more weight? Pilate thought of Tiberius Caesar, his cruel and suspicious master, and then of his own bad record of administration. Son of God! Caesar's friend! The last voice prevailed. As the evangelist dramatically puts it, "And their voice prevailed." "Shall I crucify your King?" cried Pilate. And back came the answer, "We have no king but Caesar." Caesar! That finished Pilate. He called for a basin of water, washed his hands before the people, and said, "I am innocent of the blood of this righteous man. See ye to it." Then Pilate delivered Jesus over to be crucified.

COMPARISON

Zedekiah and Pilate both knew the truth, but refused to obey it. They are both fascinating studies, and solemn and arresting, too, of how the heart of the natural man twists and turns in its effort to evade the commandment of conscience.

Both Zedekiah and Pilate were unexpectedly confronted with the prophets of God, Zedekiah with Jeremiah, and Pilate with the Son of God Himself. Zedekiah, although surrounded by false prophets and false advisers, knew that Jeremiah was the true prophet, and frequently consulted him to know what the word of God was. Yet when he heard that word he refused to do it. Pilate was convinced from the very beginning that in the solitary prisoner who was brought to his court early on that fateful Friday morning, he had to do with no ordinary person.

Zedekiah consulted Jeremiah in secret: Pilate had two private interviews with Jesus. Both men at first strove to do what conscience directed. In every possible way Pilate sought to avoid passing sentence upon Jesus. Both of them, however, compromised with wrong. Zedekiah permitted Jeremiah to be cast into the abandoned well, and Pilate, although he knew Jesus to be innocent, permitted Him to be scourged, with the hope that the hatred of the Jews would be satisfied by such a punishment.

Both were kept from doing right by the fear of man. Zedekiah was all but ready to follow the advice of Jeremiah, but drew back through fear of mockery and injury at the hands of his own people. Pilate, up to the very last, seems to be determined to set Jesus free. But when he heard someone cry, "Thou art not Caesar's friend," for fear of losing the friendship of Caesar, and his office in Judea, he delivered Jesus over to be crucified.

The last we see of Zedekiah is when he is carried, blinded and mutilated, into captivity in Babylon. Legend has been busy with the subsequent history of Pilate. One tradition tells how both Pilate and his wife, Procula, became converts to the gospel and were condemned to death by the emperor Tiberius. Another tradition says that, having been condemned by the emperor, he committed suicide. His body was thrown first into the Tiber and then into the Rhone. Both rivers refused to receive the body, and it was driven northward and sunk in Lake Lucerne. Visitors to Lucerne see the great mountain at one end of the lake which bears the name of Pilate, and hear the story, that on every Good Friday, Pilate is raised from the lake and sits on the mount unavailingly washing his hands.

In his tale, *The Procurator of Judea*, Anatole France tells of a meeting at Baiae, a fashionable Roman watering place, between a dissipated Roman, Laelius Lamia, and Pontius Pilate. The two had known each other when Pilate was governor of Judea and Lamia was living there in exile. Lamia begins to reminisce, and recalls the beauty of a Jewish dancer with whom he had been infatuated and whom he had followed about for some time, and then lost track of her. "Some months after I lost sight of her, I learned by chance that she had attached herself to a small company of men and women who were followers of a young Galilean thaumaturgist. His name was Jesus; He came from Nazareth, and He was crucified for some crime. I don't know what. Pontius, do you remember anything about the Man?"

Pontius Pilate contracted his brows, and his hand rose to his forehead in the attitude of one who probes the deeps of memory. Then, after a silence of some seconds—"Jesus," he murmured, "Jesus, . . . of Nazareth? I cannot call Him to mind."

Books by Clarence E. Macartney

Chariots of Fire
The Faith Once Delivered
The Great Characters of the Bible
The Great Interviews of the Bible
Great Women of the Bible
The Greatest Questions of the Bible and of Life
The Greatest Texts of the Bible
The Greatest Words in the Bible and in Human Speech
He Chose Twelve
The Parables of the Old Testament
Parallel Lives of the Old and New Testaments
Paul the Man
The Prayers of the Old Testament
Strange Texts but Grand Truths
12 Great Questions About Christ